Academic Community

Discourse or Discord?

To Roy Niblett
from us all

Higher Education Policy Series 20

Academic Community
Discourse or Discord?

Edited by Ronald Barnett

Jessica Kingsley Publishers
London and Bristol, Pennsylvania

First published in the United Kingdom in 1994 by
Jessica Kingsley Publishers Ltd
116 Pentonville Road
London N1 9JB, England
and
1900 Frost Road, Suite 101
Bristol, PA 19007, U S A

Copyright © 1994 the contributors and the publisher

Library of Congress Cataloging in Publication Data are available

British Library Cataloguing in Publication Data

Academic Community: Discourse or Discord?.
- (Higher Education Policy Series)
I. Barnett, Ronald II. Series
370.19

ISBN 1-85302-534-8

Printed and Bound in Great Britain by
Biddles Ltd., Guildford and King's Lynn

Contents

Acknowledgements

This volume has grown out of the 1991 annual conference of the Higher Education Foundation held in Roehampton, London. I am grateful to the Trustees of the Foundation for allowing some of those presenting papers on that occasion to use their material as the basis for their contributions to this book, that is the chapters by Tony Becher, Ruth Finnegan, Nicholas Maxwell, Christian Schumacher, Peter Scott and Kenneth Wilson.

I would also like to record my appreciation of Jessica Kingsley who supported my contention that the theme of academic community was worth exploring.

Ronald Barnett

Part I

The Idea of Academic Community

Chapter 1

Recovering an Academic Community
Above but not Beyond

Ronald Barnett

Initial bearings

In this initial chapter, I aim to do four things: first, to analyse the senses that we might give to 'academic community' and to clarify the ways in which it might be apparent; second, to identify key issues and concerns in relation to academic community; third, to offer a framework for approaching the contributions to this volume; and last, to offer a particular argument of my own.

Like 'liberal education', the term 'academic community' has almost passed out of our language. Neither lecturers nor students working, for example, in history, physics, occupational therapy and business studies find it easy or even possible to find points of contact. In their separate *Tribes and Territories* (Becher 1989), academics have their own hold on academe, their distinctive forms of life, and indeed separate culture and values. There is little sense of community and even less actual sign of community. But if those inside the university no longer seek to understand each other through the idea of academic community, neither does the wider society wish to comprehend academe through the term. The university has either become an institution for producing specialised technical capacities or is still largely an amorphous institution, the character of its internal life lacking any kind of clarity. On either count, whether internal or external views, 'academic community' drops out of the lexicon; we seem to be able to get by quite satisfactorily without it.

Two sets of questions are immediately appropriate. The first set is *factual*. What is going on here? What are the underlying changes taking place in academe so that we have become reluctant to speak without embarrassment of an 'academic community'? What are the forces at work which render 'academic community' a quaint idea of the past? The second set of questions has an explicit *value* component.

Does this shift in our vocabulary matter? Does it point to underlying changes in academic life which we might even regret?

When or if we have answers to these questions – of fact and of value – we can then turn to a third set of questions which is more constructive and even optimistic in tone. Can we hope to realise a sense of community in academe today? If so, what form or forms might it take? And under what conditions might it be sustained?

This book is an attempt to grapple with all three sets of questions. Analyses are offered of the extent to which 'community' is an idea which, in principle, has sense in relation to the academic world. Accounts are also developed of ways in which the presence of community has eroded over recent times. The general, though qualified, view is that this shift does matter: it represents a real loss. Almost every contribution, however, does not stop there but goes on to offer proposals by which an academic community might yet become a meaningful description of the academic world. The proposals take a range of forms and supply the structure of the book: community, or coherence of endeavour, can be recovered through *academic inquiry*, both in its form and in its substance; through the *curriculum*; and through the university as an *organisation*.

Most of the chapters in this volume range widely and embrace a number of dimensions of community. Many could have been placed in other sections. More than that, the three categories of analysis and possible solutions – through inquiry, curriculum and organisation – provide just one way of carving up the contributions. Other important themes figure in several chapters and might easily have formed the basis for different groupings. For example, communication, power and bridges (both within the academic world and between it and the wider society) appear as three key issues in the discussions that follow. So the ordering presented here represents just one reading of the offerings. It is, though, an ordering chosen to maximise the practical impact of the volume. Academic inquiry, the curriculum and the university as an organisation are surely the dominant modes in which academics conduct their professional livings. It is there, in those arenas, if at all, that any kind of academic community is going to be realised.

Perhaps unusually in academic debate, the contributions in this volume are characterised by their readiness to offer definite proposals for action. None is confined purely to analysis or takes on the appearance of hand-wringing. Inevitably, there is a relation between analysis and prescription: an argument that a loss of community is reflected in language leads naturally to the suggestion that it is through language that community can be recovered (see Reeves, Chapter 8).

Correspondingly, a sense that community is embodied in the university as an institution prompts the idea that our institutions as such can embrace a new form of community (see Finnegan, Chapter 12). Or the recognition that academe is composed of cognitive subcultures often seeing each other through stereotypical lenses offers the possibility that community might be forged through cross-cultural (in epistemic terms) inquiry (see Becher, Chapter 4).

Is there a problem?

It could be argued that there is no problem here. Instead, there may be an overreadiness both to misjudge the past and to misconstrue the present. There never was a golden age when we could speak without qualification of an academic community (see Scott, Chapter 2). The academic world is characterised by critical debate, by alternative viewpoints, even by fissure. To prescribe a particular, and over-arching, framework of thought is to impose an iron cage and to emasculate the point of academic inquiry. It is also to insert a dimension of power in a form of life which should be open to all comers. At the same time, the contemporary character of academe is witnessing many fruitful signs of migrations of thought and ideas across boundaries (see Becher, Chapter 4). So things are not so bad as they seem; while the whole project of searching for unifying principles will threaten the very basis of academic life.

In this chapter, I want directly to tackle that argument, but before I do so, let us try to understand the significance of the issue in front of us. Understanding its significance may give us clues as to how to tackle it.

Even if there is a problem over academic community, why should it matter? Higher education and the academic life are still minority activities. And provided open warfare is not breaking out, does it matter if the academics do not enjoy a complete sense of community with each other?

The first response is that while higher education remains (in most countries) a minority activity, it is still a sizeable enterprise consuming much public resource and effort. Further, although a minority activity in terms of the numbers of people involved, the significance of higher education is undeniable. No country of any size is without its universities. The university occupies a pivotal place in modern society: it is both symptomatic of modern society and a harbinger of that society. Modern society is built around formal knowledge and the human capacities to understand, to handle and to continue to transform that knowledge. The university is bound up precisely with those societal functions.

These are quasi-pragmatic responses. The second set of responses is more conceptual but follows on. The cognitive structure of modern society is reflected in the academy. The forms of knowledge and their associated experiences made available in academe are not happenstance but constitute a particular ordering, a selection, from the infinite possible variety of forms of human cognition. To a significant extent, the available forms of cognition are those summoned forth by society. As society changes, so does its cognitive demands on the university. Transferable skills (see Griffin, Chapter 9) are just one example of society's changing expectations of the university. And if it is said that that is just a UK example, not to be found elsewhere, that is because of the contemporary relationships between higher education and the state in the UK. But the example has more general resonances: modern society is one of change and graduates are being called for who are 'flexible', able to make something of their cognitive capital throughout the challenges and changes of their careers and, indeed, to go on renewing that cognitive capital itself.

All of this is to say that if there is a lack of community of some sort in our universities, that must begin to say something about community in the wider society. It cannot be the case that cognitive structures are falling apart in the academy but are holding together in society more generally. The modern academy is an institution both *in* and *of* society. Its forms of thought are to be found, living with their own dynamic, across society. They are not the only forms of thought of society but they are forms of thought which are constituent of modernity, as felt by society. 'Academic' forms of thought are not just academic but are partly constitutive of society. If there are tensions across forms of thought and experience in the university, those tensions have to be present in society.

The point can be put another way with some force. There would be a wide, if not general, consensus that the world faces many grave problems (see Maxwell, Chapter 6). Some are connected with an unequal distribution of power and resources and will require sociopolitical solutions. Many, however, and including perhaps all of the first category, are partly or mainly cognitive in character. Problems of ecology and of the environment, of malnutrition, of social order, of economy, of social welfare and of the form and distribution of employment: all of these and many others will require the combination and integration of the planet's intellectual resources if they are to be tackled in any kind of adequate way. Further, the deployment of intellectual resources will be insufficient in itself. The intellectual discourse has to come into contact with and be generally comprehended by *and* informed by the wider discourses of society. In the end, society's problems have to be attacked by society collectively.

It follows that if there are doubts about the extent to which the academic community can be said to be a community, this is a matter with implications beyond academe. If the discourses of academe are breaking apart, if academics have difficulty not only in understanding each other but in finding a way of communicating with each other, this has to have impact on and in the wider society. Academic languages are not only to be found in the university but wash over into society; and are used in society. A loss of community among academics has to result in a loss of community in the wider society.

The idea of academic community

So far, we have been talking in a fairly undifferentiated way about academic community. Yet the term is ambiguous and warrants some clarification. The term might mean that:

1. the discourses of academics, in their disciplinary groupings, are increasingly distinct and separate

2. academics have for some time been identified with separate disciplines but now are less able to recognise one another as being involved in a common enterprise

3. academics, being now expected to generate much of their own income, are increasingly competitive against each other

4. in a higher education system which is increasingly evaluated, academics become concerned mainly with their own affairs and are less interested in the activities of academics in other departments

5. as institutions are having to become more efficient, and work with lower unit costs, individuals concentrate on their own activities and are less inclined to work cooperatively with others in groups or departments

6. as modular and credit accumulation systems develop, the curriculum becomes unitised, the individual units being separate from each other: in that context, the experience of students and the work of academics as teachers also becomes fragmented

7. in an age characterised by instrumentalism, students have their eye on their hoped-for careers and see their higher education in instrumental terms. It becomes a form of work, undertaken for an external end in a private mode. Consequently, the communal aspects of student life lessen,

and students across disciplines feel themselves to have less in common with each other

8. as students become 'customers', exerting their individual claims on institutions, again the student experience becomes more differentiated as institutions respond to the different claims of students across the disciplines.

There are three perspectives among these different interpretations of loss of community:

1. community as discourse or language, a loss of community being felt in a new kind of inability to communicate within the academic world

2. community as institutional interaction, a loss of community being evident in academic institutions

3. community as a function of the student experience, a loss of community being apparent in the student body.

These three forms of community are both conceptually and empirically separate from each other. We can imagine any one being present independent of the others. There *could* be a loss of community among the students even while the academics retained theirs. The academics *might* be gaining a new sense of working cooperatively in the life of their institutions – for example, in developing a staff appraisal system or a course evaluation system – at the very time when their disciplinary subcultures were breaking further apart. Also, with the flow and dynamic of disciplinary cultures, of universities as institutions, and of the changing character of national systems of higher education, one or other of the three forms of community (or its loss) may claim our attention at one moment to give way in the next decade to another form of community.

Another way of clarifying the meaning – or, better, the range of meanings – of a complex term is to identify the constellation of other terms or concepts that are typically associated with it (Bernstein 1991). What, we may ask, is the conceptual company that it keeps? And here, as we have already seen, typical of the terms accompanying 'academic community', at least in the offerings in this volume, are:

- fragmentation: Wyatt, Schumacher
- (in)coherence: Becher, Wyatt, Schumacher, Scott, Wilson
- language: Reeves, Wilson
- communication: Wilson, Finnegan, Schumacher, Reeves, Roberts

- bridging the academic and the wider world: Niblett, Griffin, Wilson, Maxwell, Roberts
- power: Scott, Becher, Finnegan, Reeves, Schumacher
- metadiscourse or unifying principles of discourse: Becher, Finnegan, Scott, Reeves, Wyatt, Wilson.

This short list alone suggests that underlying these concerns over academic community is a problem over communication structures in academe. But there are, as Niblett's chapter reminds us, different communication structures at work in academe.

Crucial to the arguments in this volume are these communication structures:

- student–student
- lecturer–student
- lecturer–lecturer
- lecturer–administration
- academics–state bureaucracies
- academics–wider society.

These communication structures are different orders of communication built around different tasks: pedagogic, research, organisation and the development of civil society. They contain different motivations and logics. If the communication structure is distorted or fragmented in any of these six levels, it will require a particular and appropriate strategy if any improvement is to be brought off.

When it is being said, then, that we face a loss of academic community, or that higher education is fragmenting, we are entitled to ask what precisely is meant. Yet, while we can note that talk of 'academic community' is often imprecise and that several possible meanings are often not disentangled, there are also more general considerations at stake.

Academic community and culture

A sense of academic fragmentation is not new. For example, it was evident in Germany at the turn of the century, as Fritz Ringer in a recent work observes:

> The sense of loss among German (academics) was particularly deep... they feared not only intellectual fragmentation or cognitive incoherence, but also the collapse of personal, evaluative and integral knowledge. They firmly expected *Wissenschaft* to yield *Bildung* and *Weltanschauung*... A further expectation they inher-

ited from their tradition was that the universities and *Wissenschaft* would have considerable authority and influence within the larger society... They saw themselves as sages, not as specialists. (Ringer 1992)

These observations from Ringer are instructive for more than one reason. First, we see that there is often a belief on the part of the academics that the different features of its being a community are connected. Scholarship and inquiry, the formation of knowledge (*Wissenschaft*), was expected to lead to personal development (*Bildung*) and to a deeper and integrated outlook (*Weltanschauung*). We should also remember that in the German tradition, in conception at least, students were counted as scholars so these ideas applied to the students as well as to the professors.

Second, Ringer points to the wider context within which a sense of fragmentation was generated. The loss was experienced in a climate of diminished authority in the wider society. Ringer points out that:

the theme of lost authority... was often sounded when German university professors wrote about their social and political environment after 1890. It seemed to many of them that the world was increasingly dominated by blind economic processes, by the power of money, and by the weight of numbers. 'Mind' appeared to have lost its influence in public life...

Taken together, these are extraordinary passages. A commentary on German intellectual life of one hundred years ago, they will seem to many to be an apt description of higher education in the UK today. But if these remarks have force, that must be because the relevant features of the contemporary world – the 'economic processes', 'the power of money', 'the weight of numbers' (whether in terms of student numbers or numerical performance indicators in evaluation procedures) and the loss of 'mind' – are now *felt* to be significant by at least a sizeable proportion of the academic world.

Institutions and groups look to strengthen their own inner ties when under some kind of perceived threat. So too with academics. Talk of a loss of academic community is not new, therefore. It breaks out when there is a marked disjunction between the interests of the academic world on the one hand and the perceptions of the academics of the demands of the wider world upon them. It marks a sense of threat or diminished authority on the part of the academics. It is an indication that the academics feel the need to reidentify what it is they have in common and to reassert their distinctive identity in and contribution to society. Concerns over academic community turn out, then, to be a symptom of that community's weakened position in society. A community or grouping does not worry over its inner connections and identities when it is flourishing and when its constituent parts are confident.

Yet there is more to be said. Concerns over academic community are not *just* a matter of perceptions on the part of some academics. The contributions to this volume do express such concerns but to discount them as simply perceptions (perhaps not widely shared across all disciplines) or as merely expressions of self-interest on the part of the academic community would be to fail to take seriously their collective significance.

Concerns of this kind do not just occur. As in Germany at the turn of the century and successively since, they are a response to real happenings in the world. The dominant interests in money, in economic processes, in the use of numbers: to these contemporary characteristics of the operating environment of the academic world (present in Ringer's analysis of Germany) we can add more recent interests in learning as 'outcomes', in the transformation of universities into hierarchical organisations with chief executives, in systems for 'accountability' and in curriculum reorganisation conducted as a top-down exercise. All of these are ways in which the professional authority of academics is being challenged and, indeed, in which their academic freedom is being curtailed.

The point here is not, however, one about academic freedom or institutional organisation. It is that these sensitivities are indicative of a disjunction in culture between the academic world and the wider society.

Expressions of concern over academic community are an attempt on the part of the academic world to identify and reassert the values and unifying ties which bind it together, and which differentiate it from the perceived values of the wider world. It is hardly surprising, therefore, if we find such concerns being voiced at a moment when, as now, higher education is being urged to take on the values and concerns of the wider society and its operating procedures. Higher education is being told: be like us, have our values, and in fact become part of us. Indeed, it is being told: for too long, you have been apart from us, holding yourself distinct and separate. In future, you must become one of society's institutions, responsive to its claims and expectations. Far from the formation of the student mind having a character independent of society, now the student formation is to be precisely a function of occupational requirements specified as 'competences' and sought as 'learning outcomes' (Jessup 1991). In short, the university is to be entirely incorporated into the institutional apparatus of modern society.

At the root of concerns over academic community, therefore, are fundamental matters of culture and of the relationships between the university and the wider society. How do we understand the culture of the academic world? Is it distinctive? Is it different from the dominant culture of mainstream society? Is there a culture that we can claim to be characteristic of the academic enterprise, independent of the traditions and styles of cognition and procedure to be found in the separate disciplines? If there is such a culture, to what extent is it being threatened by an assimilation into the culture of modernity?

To pose such questions, of course, raises others. For example, does a phrase like 'the culture of modernity' have real cash value? Isn't modern society, or at least postmodern society, characterised by being a collection of different cultures? And in that case, what does the claimed-for threat amount to? Being assimilated into a postmodern world, and even being part of it already, suggests that far from cognitive and intellectual constraint being the order of the day, pretty well anything goes (Feyerabend 1978). But that is far too sanguine a view of what is happening. The empirical realities of incorporation into the state apparatus are clear and significant. The important questions remain: is there anything we can point to which amounts to an academic culture worth identifying and preserving? Is it under any kind of threat, if not of direct attack then of gradual dissipation through assimilation?

Academic community in an age of postmodernity

As we have observed, talk of academic community sometimes seems to be an expression of nostalgia for a golden age of community that never was (see Scott, Chapter 2). And we have seen why. Such talk emerges at a moment of perceived external threat. In the postmodern world, however, such talk *itself* can appear to verge on the side of illegitimate constraint. From one perspective, at least, talk of 'academic community' represents an attempt to find principles of cognitive and intellectual constraint.

Postmodernism delights in perspectival proliferation. If *that* is the character of the academic world, if as its disciplinary communities split apart, there are no overarching principles of right reason, that is a matter for rejoicing. On one reading, the university was a postmodern institution before its time. Ever since the late nineteenth century, it has been a holding company for quite different kinds of cognitive activity. At best, 'university' meant openness to forms of knowing, if, at times, reluctantly; in its modern form, it could not mean a single universe of knowledge. The disciplines developed their own conceptual frameworks, truth criteria, modes of discourse and operating procedures (Hirst 1965). They became distinctive forms of academic life. Nor, for postmodernism, is this situation to be regretted. On the contrary, this very epistemic egalitarianism is a symptom of the openness celebrated *by* postmodernism.

From this point of view, postmodernism – with its multiple realities – is genuinely liberating. The apparent reasonableness of western rationality was always a form of cognitive domination in which claims to know were brought against narrow criteria of reason, especially those embodied first in science and then in technology. Seen in this light, the wide range of cognitive options open to the modern student can only be welcomed. Now that there are no supreme cognitive judges, all manner of intellectual pursuits can justifiably be conducted alongside each other.

There are, though, faults with this analysis; and, again, the student, academic and administrative levels of community may be helpful here. Let us start at the level of the curriculum and the student experience.

The ability on the part of the student to make informed choices between cognitive options presupposes a sufficient understanding of the alternatives. This cannot be gained by the student's pursuit of a narrow programme of studies built around a single discipline. But neither is informed choice a likely outcome of the current alternatives.

Professional programmes structured around a number of disciplines have breadth but they tend to be tightly constrained, the greater part of the programme being determined by the relevant professional body. On the other hand, modular programmes have a higher degree of openness but that very openness can lead to a relatively superficial encounter with the conceptual structures of the underlying disciplines of a student's programme. We have taken on the language of an educational market, in which students are customers but it is doubtful that students can ever really exercise informed choice. After all, the discourse of the academics in their journals and conferences is very often at a remove from the discourse present in undergraduate curricula that they teach. In some disciplines, it is said, 'real work' is not undertaken until the PhD, if then. In a specialised academic world, the undergraduate is barely able to get on the inside of a single discipline, let alone experience to any serious level alternative epistemic ways of seeing the world.

Second, and still at the level of the student experience, simply doing one's thing, intellectually at least, cannot amount to an educational experience. Being no longer held in thrall to narrow assumptions of 'a great tradition', we may widen to infinity the forms of cognitive experience allowable within higher education. Kitsch culture vies with high culture; and all hierarchies are open to interpretation (cf. Gless and Smith 1992). 'Some postmodernists look with nostalgia on the past...a few even romanticize the period when people lived in caves. The postmodern "remembers, recollects" and asserts that there is no special value for the new' (Rosenau 1992). But unless students are given the conceptual wherewithal to stand back, interpret and criticise their experience – in whatever subject – it is difficult to see how it can justifiably lay claim to being a *higher* education.

The problem is that, in the end, the extreme tolerance of postmodernism denies critical standards. Since postmodernism denies the existence of absolute criteria of reason, it is unclear how evaluation of truth claims can ever get a purchase. All we have are different forms of life, different modes of thought and different perspectives. Truth criteria, presumably, are simply internal to a discourse. This is not unsettling in itself, but what is the status of those internalist criteria? On what basis do they count as truth criteria as distinct from a collective whim in a particular subgroup? This is not a point about relativism, but a point about the basis of intellectual discourse. At least relativism has a theory of truth: that is that group's truth and this is this group's. In its radical form, postmodernism seems even to deny the very attribution of truth.

This matters for the student experience. Students may enjoy their disciplinary experience for its own sake, but that experience will be a form of entrapment rather than emancipation unless students are enabled to see into the interests and presuppositions of their chosen subject; and for that they need to take on the principles of critical reason. Postmodernism, far from freeing one from dependency, legitimises separate frameworks and in the process robs higher education of its critical stance for disciplines have to be taken as given.

Recovering general principles of community

Postmodernism is surely right in its denial of the security of overarching intellectual narratives (Lyotard 1987). The notion of academic community cannot be saved by importing a common mission in which the western university is expected to be involved. Universities have many different missions. So-called mission statements are either a statement of the trite and bland, failing to demarcate different activities of institutions, or they are so detailed and specific that, if taken seriously, they would impede the autonomy of an institution's academic staff. (Fortunately, they seldom are taken seriously.) Missions cannot be imposed on communities; missions will develop organically out of communities. That is the nature of genuine communities, as distinct from organisations (MacIntyre 1982).

If, therefore, general principles are to be identified which are both general in nature and do justice to the activities of academics (to which *they* are committed), such principles have already to be implicit in academic activities in all their differentiated forms. An account along these lines is suggested by the work of Jurgen Habermas.

Habermas argues that western rationality is an unfinished project (White 1989, Rasmussen 1990). Its dominant forms may have limitations, springing from an underlying interest in prediction and control; but it contains within itself forms of rationality and communication not yet fully realised. The idea of reason, Habermas argues, is posited in the use of language oriented to truth. That is to say, locked within any serious claim to know part of the world or advance an argument are certain procedural principles which make possible a rational discourse. In order to get a discourse going which is intended to be more than a discourse and to yield some understanding in the recipient, certain principles of rational discourse have to be upheld. It cannot be the case, on this view, that 'anything goes': anarchy is not an option since, if anything of substance is to be said, a number of ethical and validity claims have to be made by any speaker.

We should not abandon prematurely, therefore, the belief in a universal discourse. It may be embedded in the deep structure of intellectual life as such and, if so, that is the common enterprise into which we induct our students. The common culture of the academic community, if it exists at all, is to be found in the universal principles of reason and communication binding on all those seriously interested at getting at truth (see Becher, Chapter 4). It is, to use a shorthand borrowed from Alvin Gouldner, a culture of critical discourse (Gouldner 1979).

If there is anything in this line of approach, there are two consequences for higher education. First, to be clearer about the universal conditions of rational discourse and to make them explicit in the teaching process. As a first shot (drawing partly on Habermas), we might say that any rational discourse demands of its users: sincerity, comprehensibility, appropriateness, veracity, care, honesty, sympathetic listening, a willingness to examine matters from different points of view, respect for participants' positions in a dialogue, and persistence – a determination to get to the bottom of things (cf. Habermas 1979). If qualities of this kind are intrinsic to and, therefore, universally to be found across the academic life, we should be prepared to state them explicitly to our students. They should know, in other words, not just X and Y, or even reasons for X and Y, but what it is for them to make claims about X and Y. In this way (to take a phrase from Shils), they come to understand the academic ethic (Shils 1983).

Second, if there is a universal culture of rational discourse in academic life of this kind, we have to find ways of imparting it so that our programmes of study are effective in developing the relevant general qualities (as well as any subject-specific qualities we have in mind) (see Finnegan, Chapter 12). The implied independence of thought and the cognitive distance suggest two strategies.

First, the teaching process should employ various kinds of open learning which demand of the student that he or she takes up and develops an intellectual position in the company of, and subject to, the supportive but critical commentary of his or her peers. Second, forms of interdisciplinarity are surely necessary if the students are to gain the necessary intellectual detachment from their main studies (see Becher, Chapter 4). And such elements, even if for a minority of their work, could form a vehicle for students in different subject areas to come together. To be taken seriously, the elements would have to be assessed.

The second mode in which academic community might be developed is that of academic inquiry. This issue is analysed in some depth by Tony Becher in his contribution and I shall, therefore, content myself with some general remarks.

We noted earlier (p4) that among the conceptual and empirical strands closely related to academic community is that of power. It is evident in the sphere of academic inquiry. Conceptual schemes or discourses become organisations of power (Foucault 1980): organised, institutionalised knowledge is a power structure, buttressed and defended by those on the inside. From this perspective, it is hardly surprising if adherents to a particular epistemic discourse find it difficult to collaborate with those in another discourse. To do so leads to a diminution in one's exercise of power.

We have to ask: is the academic organisation of knowledge into disciplines necessary? What is the character of the academic division of labour? If disciplines thwart communication across disciplines and academic institutions, can we do without them? From time to time, different orderings of knowledge have been tried in universities. Usually, but not always, it has needed the opportunity of establishing a new institution: witness Keele (Gallie 1960), Sussex (Daiches 1964), the Open University (see Finnegan, Chapter 12); Chicago in the 1930s, however, was different with the arrival of a new young principal, Robert Hutchins. On each occasion, attempts were made to bring disciplines into some kind of relationship with each other; and, so far as can be judged, with some success. Community in academic inquiry may still just be a possibility.

Some segmentation of knowledge is probably inevitable. Most academics are comfortable identifying with a certain cluster of problems and ideas and are uncomfortable with others. They will want to keep intellectual company with others of like orientation. But this is not to determine any particular ordering. Rather, the issue is more: how do we keep lines of communication open with any particular ordering that we currently have? After all, it is in the academics' own interest. Many of the interesting lines of intellectual development arise precisely through the importation or migration of ideas from one field to another (see Scott, Chapter 2). And many of those who are innovators in one field are those who are able to straddle more than one field or at least be aware of developments other than in their current home discipline.

My earlier point about the relationship between knowledge and power suggests that an adequate answer to this issue will be found through the organisation of academic inquiry. It follows that the development of an academic community – in the sphere of academic inquiry – is a challenge to institutional managers. It is unclear, however, whether institutional managers will wish to respond positively to the problem. This takes us to our next mode of interaction in which academic community can show itself.

The third level is that of the administrative sphere. Again, the element of power is present. Whether we have in mind administration at institutional level or at national level, it can be plausibly argued that far from wanting academics to act as a community a policy of divide-and-rule is administratively attractive. Such a policy maximises the exercise of power at the centre. Certainly, this is a possible reading of the quality assessment exercise being mounted by the Higher Education Funding Council for England. There, the quality of programmes offered in institutions are to be assessed against each other and separately from each other (HEFCE 1993). Not surprisingly, it appears (at the moment of writing) that the universities might try to scupper the policy by all declaring their programmes of excellent quality, so trying to making its operation from the centre unmanageable. Whatever the outcome, here we have an attempt to keep institutions separate from each other, a policy which has had the reverse effect of uniting universities. A *community* of interests and mode of interacting with the state's apparatus arises as an unintended consequence of a policy carrying the opposite intention.

Within institutions, the relationship between the administrative sphere and academic community is less clear. Again, a motivation is present to encourage operating units to compete against each other, if only to drive up efficiency. On the other hand, curriculum developments such as modular systems and the establishment of internal evaluation procedures actually require cross-faculty visibility and cooperation if they are to work. Many new programmes which institutional managers wish to encourage – for example, in tourism, or European studies, or in the health professions – also range widely across disciplines and require colleagues across parts of the university to work together. So academic community can be promoted in the administrative sphere.

Conclusion: above but not beyond

Modern society is fragmenting and, with it, its discourses and self-understandings. The fragmentation of academic discourse both reflects this societal fragmentation and reinforces it. Rather than the rationality of society growing, it appears to be reducing. Unless academe acts to counter this limited rationality and fragmentation of understanding in society, it will be cast in the role of an accomplice in these large movements of the age.

We have seen that there are various meanings that can be given to academic community. It can be found at different levels in academe, involving different subcommunities (including students and administrative bureaucracies) and is oriented around different kinds of discourse with different motivations (pedagogic, academic and administrative). Strains on academic community can be found at all of these levels and in all of these discourses. There are, though, a general set of conclusions which suggest themselves.

No principles can be plucked out of the air which can unify the academic community. First, secure foundations will not be available (Rorty 1980). Second, the academic life is marked by its independence and inner dynamic: however attractive to some, super narratives will have few takers. From time to time, small groups may subscribe to a new logic or paradigm; but it would amount to an abandonment of its raison d'être for the academic class as a whole to fall in behind newly-identified general principles of thought.

Yet, to repeat, it is not the case – despite Feyerabend's pleas – that anything goes. All academic modes of functioning have to respect certain rules which characterise any discourse oriented towards truth. Rules such as truthfulness, comprehensibility, sincerity, appropriateness, receptiveness and orderliness are built into academic discourse in any of its modes, and in any of its forms. It would not be right to say – as postmodernists sometimes do – that such rules are constraining. On the contrary, these rules make rational critical discourse possible. They are the underpinning of academic discourse.

If this is plausible – and it is implied in the modern variant of Critical Theory in the work of Jurgen Habermas – then identifying the rules of academic discourse is a matter of reminding the academic community of its existing basis. It is also to bring out the character of rational discourse as such.

Learning and living by the rules of rational discourse is more important than getting on the inside of any particular subvariant in the form of a discipline. This is worth doing not only for the sake of the academic community or even for the sake of the students who pass through academe. Rather, it is worth doing for the sake of the wider society. Reminding the academic groupings of their common constitutive rules can help to promote a renewed sense of academic community. But identifying these constitutive rules of rational discourse can also assist in promoting the level of rationality of modern society (Habermas 1972).

The essential discourse of academe, then, turns out to be a metadiscourse, consisting of the rules of rational discourse. These are higher order rules than the local rules of the fields of academic life. Yet, while being higher order rules of discourse, they are not separable from the constitution of society. If society is to be fully rational, those higher order rules have to permeate institutional life generally. Above they may be, but not beyond.

References

Becher, T. (1989) *Academic Tribes and Territories*. Milton Keynes: Open University Press.

Bernstein, R.J. (1991) *The New Constellation*. Cambridge: Polity Press.

Daiches, D. (ed) (1964) *The Idea of a New University*. London: Deutsch.

Feyerabend, P. (1978) *Against Method*. London: Verso.

Foucault, M. (1980) *Power/Knowledge*. Hemel Hempstead: Wheatsheaf Harvester.

Gallie, W.B. (1960) *A New University: A D Lindsay and the Keele Experiment*. London: Chatto and Windus.

Gless, D. and Smith, B.H. (eds) (1992) *The Politics of Liberal Education*. Durham, USA: Duke University Press.

Gouldner, A. (1979) *The Future of Intellectuals and the Rise of the New Class*. London: Macmillan.

Habermas, J. (1972) *Towards a Rational Society*. London: Heinemann.

Habermas, J. (1979) *Communication and the Evolution of Society.* London: Heinemann.

HEFCE (1993) *Assessment of the Quality of Education,* Circular 3/93. Bristol: Higher Education Funding Council for England.

Hirst, P. (1965) Liberal Education and the Nature of Knowledge. In R.G. Archambault (ed) *Philosophical Analysis and Education.* London: Routledge and Kegan Paul.

Jessup, G. (1991) *Outcomes: NVQs and the Emerging Model of Education and Training.* London: Falmer.

Lyotard, J.F. (1987) *The Postmodern Condition: A Report on Knowledge.* Manchester: Manchester University Press.

MacIntyre, A. (1982) *After Virtue.* London: Duckworth.

Ringer, F. (1992) *Fields of Knowledge: French Academic Culture in Comparative Perspective, 1890–1920.* Cambridge: Cambridge University Press.

Rasmussen, D. (1990) *Reading Habermas.* Oxford: Blackwell.

Rorty, R. (1980) *Philosophy and the Mirror of Nature.* Oxford: Blackwell.

Rosenau, P.M. (1992) *Postmodernism and the Social Sciences: Insights, Inroads and Intrusions.* Chichester: Princeton University Press.

Shils, E. (1983) *The Academic Ethic.* London: University of Chicago.

White, S.K. (1989) *The Recent Work of Jurgen Habermas: Reason, Justice and Modernity.* Cambridge: Cambridge University Press.

Chapter 2

Divide and Rule

Peter Scott

Introduction: appearance and reality

Within the academic community, the dominant language seems to be of longing and regret. One reason for this is superficial, although powerful. Rightly or wrongly, universities feel they are under attack. This attack has been on several fronts. Budgets have been cut or, at any rate, failed to keep place with inflation and the expansion of student numbers. As more students have crowded into higher education, the conditions of academic work have deteriorated. Collegiality has been undermined by competition. And the academic tradition has come under pressure; the life of the mind is no longer admired.

But another, more fundamental, reason for this language of regret is a pervasive defensiveness. Not only does the academic community suspect that society no longer accords it appropriate respect, it also half-fears it has lost faith in its own values. This decline in intellectual, and moral, self-confidence helps to explain the retrospective mentality that affects large parts of the academic community. The gaze is backwards to Arcadia, not forwards to Utopia. There is a memorable image in George Steiner's book *Real Presences* of the modern condition – we feel the setting sun on our backs, a final whiff of warmth, as we look into the impenetrable gloom of the approaching night; the best, we instinctively feel, is behind us (Steiner 1989). This recessional mood, so palpable, has to be taken into account in any serious discussion of the theme of this book – academic community: discourse or discord? Its pervasiveness affects, perhaps infects, our definitions of each word – academic, community, discourse and discord.

Modernity: a force for fragmentation

The aim of this chapter is to discuss the consequences of academic disintegration for our political culture and for modern society; hence

its title, 'Divide and Rule'. Optimists (for there are some even in the
encircling gloom) may object to the phrase 'academic disintegration',
preferring instead to describe the diversity of contemporary intellectual life as a healthy, even creative, pluralism. Yet dispersal – to adopt
a word midway between the pessimism of disintegration and the
optimism of diversity – is an aspect of modern intellectual culture
that cannot be denied, although it demands careful analysis. Nor can
the question it provokes: does this disintegration/dispersal/diver-
sity make it more difficult to maintain free institutions and sustain a
tradition of free inquiry, on which both a democratic way of life and
progressive science ultimately depend? Or, on the contrary, does it
lead ineluctably to a society of 'experts', with only feeble communication between them, and presided over by an élite bound together
by managerial rather than liberal values?

The instinct of many in the academic community, accustomed to
the language of 'lost content', is to believe the latter, concluding that
the undermining of a liberal culture is the consequence of an ever
finer division of intellectual labour which has made common discourse difficult or even impossible. So discord it must be. And the
causal link between intellectual division and cultural discord is clear
and direct. But perhaps this is an instinct, and therefore a conclusion,
that should be mistrusted. Under modern (or postmodern?) conditions, striving for coherence and commonality may produce reductionist and even oppressive effects, the very opposite of those the
liberal project is designed to foster, while the incoherence and disintegration dreaded by so many may free the intellectual imagination
to rove more widely and without constraint, perhaps ultimately
achieving a higher order integration.

My preference is for this latter account, although it is a preference
that must be argued for in the face of the powerful and, for many in
the academic community, persuasive Arcadianism which has just
been described. But the liberal civilisation which we so much admire
and instinctively feel is under threat was never the calm, ordered
Augustan culture remembered by today's Arcadians. Instead, it was
intimately related to the growth of industrial society, with all its
disturbing socio-economic reverberations, and also to patterns of
thought characterised as 'modernism', with even more alarming
consequences for the way the world, natural and human, is perceived
and valued. In other words, liberal civilisation, in its birth and
continued life, was a radical force. It made true conservatism impossible. And, by means of a permanent revolution of self-criticism and
self-subversion, this liberal culture has continued to renew its vital
energies. Historically its association has been far more with destruc-
tion, and renewal, than with continuity and coherence.

This sense of the radicalism of liberal civilisation may be difficult to recapture today. But it was clearly seen by those who first encountered the new liberal-industrial culture, fondly recalling the solidities and certainties of pre-industrial society with its endlessly recurring, and reassuring, rhythms. Coleridge's idea of 'clerisy', a secular priesthood which would continue to impose a moral order on the volatility of modern society, was a deliberate device to discipline and even curb these new and disturbing energies. Carlyle, amazed and alarmed by industrialism, wrote of men becoming mechanical. Hegel wrote in the preface to the second edition of *Science and Logic* about 'the peculiar restlessness and dispersion of our modern consciousness', a sentiment more to be expected from some contemporary analyst of postmodernism than from an early nineteenth century philosopher.

The modern scientific tradition itself is rooted in a radical scepticism. According to Thomas Kuhn, it is marked by the rise and fall of grand paradigms as one scientific value-system is superseded by another that is not so much 'truer' as incommensurable because of new social, economic and cultural circumstances (Kuhn 1962). In Karl Popper's schema, science is built up by a process of progressive falsification, as theories and interpretations are successively undermined by superior examples, although he regards falsification as a creative rather than destructive process. Even the pattern of what Kuhn calls 'normal science', routine incremental research, places a low value on integration, harmony and coherence *across* viewpoints. Instead its approach is overwhelmingly reductionist. This, therefore, is the volatile, even violent, intellectual environment of liberal civilisation from its very beginnings. It is not a recent phenomenon.

The belief that a unified and organic discourse is being undermined and the fear that the intellectual centre will not hold are not new. They go back at least as far as the end of the eighteenth century, when a distinctively modern consciousness was first forged, and have been obsessively reiterated during the intervening two centuries. They are woven into the fabric of high Victorian debates about culture. The question, therefore, is: are these diurnal feelings and fears more intense or better justified today than they were when T. S. Eliot wrote *Notes towards a Definition of Culture* (Eliot 1948) or F. R. Leavis wrote *Mass Civilisation and Minority Culture* a decade earlier (Leavis 1930) or when Carlyle wrote *Shooting Niagara* more than a century ago (Carlyle 1867)? It is difficult to answer in the unambiguous affirmative. Is the alleged unravelling of liberal civilisation – a far less coherent set of values than conventional rhetoric suggests – really as threatening a phenomenon as the collapse of religious faith in the nineteenth century?

Modernity and rationalisation

In any case, despite its diversity and fragmentation, the culture of modernity, which is perhaps another way to describe the liberal civilisation we so much admire and feel is under threat, has always had a capacity for enslavement at least as powerful as its potential for enlightenment and emancipation. Rationality, its central value, leads on to rationalisation which in turn can breed standardisation difficult to distinguish from regimentation. Modern society began to take on its present shape at the end of the eighteenth and beginning of the nineteenth centuries. This is a long-felt tension, not an exceptional contradiction of the late twentieth century. Despite the rapid advances of science since then, the immense sophistication of technology, and the transformation of political and socio-economic orders, its intellectual substructure has changed little. It was at this time that the patterns of thought identified as typically modern first evolved, that the antiphony between the individual, both as a rational and passionate being, and the mass-manufactured structures of a new society was first heard.

The capacity – indeed the necessity – for the complex organisation of industrial society is clear. Equally clear is the fact that this complex organisation has always been experienced as oppressive by many of those caught up in successive industrial revolutions. It is not an accident that many early revolutionary movements that attempted to resist industrialism were characterised by a curious mixture of millenarianism and nostalgia. 'Back to the future' was a political programme long before it became a film title! Although it is wrong to idealise pre-industrial society, the experience of individuals swept up into mass organisations often led to profound alienation. Old patterns of identity were disrupted. Nor were these changes confined to the world of work. The development of democracy was shadowed by the growth of bureaucracy; the two had, and have, to go together. But individuals experienced these changes in complex ways, at once empowered and powerless. All this was done in the name of liberal civilisation.

The same ambiguity pervaded intellectual life. Despite science's frequent and violent ruptures, its pursuit became institutionalised and professionalised, phenomena still regarded as disturbing but which had early beginnings. In *The Poverty of Historicism* Popper discussed the difficulties of combining what he called 'holistic planning', an inevitable expression of the desire to impose rational schemes of society, with the development of a critical scientific tradition, another expression of the same urge to rationality (Popper 1957). While it is possible, although undesirable, to centralise power, it is impossible to centralise knowledge which inevitably is distributed over many individual minds. His conclusion was stark: 'The greater the gain in power,' he wrote, 'the greater will be the loss of knowledge.'

Popper, of course, had in mind external, politically-inspired, interference with the free production of knowledge. But it can be argued that the very processes of institutionalisation and professionalisation, which are central to knowledge production in modern society, are also exercises in planning. Through them, for example, it is decided which people (and in which settings) are 'licensed' to conduct research. As a result, knowledge is no longer distributed across many individual minds; instead its highly uneven distribution is determined by multiple factors, many of which are closely related to the exercise of power and privilege. So, in practice, there is often a tension between the organisation and elaboration of science and the maintenance of a tradition of free intellectual inquiry.

Knowing and power

The difficulty goes even deeper. At a conceptual level, the richness and complexity of modern thought has encouraged the growth of grand theories, or metadiscourses. The most visible examples, but not necessarily the best, have been Marxism, Freudianism, Keynesianism and so on. But the academic world is littered with more discreet metadiscourses; every discipline has one or two. These interpretative frameworks are needed to reduce the explosion of knowledge to some kind of intellectual order, while at the same time this exploding knowledge provides the raw material out of which overarching theories are constructed. So grand theory both enables and disables; it enables us to achieve a more penetrating understanding of the world by offering a context of meaningfulness (even or, maybe, especially if this context is contested) but it disables because, in time, all grand theory ossifies into dispiriting orthodoxy. The grand metadiscourses of the modern world start by prescribing ideas and end by proscribing them.

As has just been argued, this ambiguity is not confined to grand intellectual systems like Marxism and Freudianism, which tend to transcend conventional academic categories and to take on a quasi-metaphysical aspect. It is present in all intellectual activity, even the most routine. According to Basil Bernstein, 'historically and now, only a tiny percentage of the population has been socialized into knowledge at the level of the meta-languages of control and innovation, whereas the mass of the population has been socialized into knowledge at the level of context-tied operation' (Bernstein 1971). In other words metadiscourses are essentially the intellectual property of élites.

Or, as Marx put it in more hard-edged terms in *The German Ideology*, 'the class that has the means of material production at its disposal has control at the same time over the means of mental production so that, generally speaking, the ideas of those who lack the means of mental production are subject to it' (Marx 1965). In an age of rampant commodification of the mass media, themselves more pervasive than ever before as a result of advances in the technology of telecommunications, this analysis appears thoroughly up to date. But this is an argument that will not be pursued here. The point being emphasised is simpler and more limited. The history of modern thought is not always or inevitably one of onwards-and-upwards emancipation; it has a dark side too, manipulative and oppressive.

What common culture? What loss?

Against this background, it becomes more difficult to persist in some key assumptions that are often made in the debate about possible threats to liberal civilisation. One of these assumptions is that at some 'golden time' in the past (when exactly is undetermined) there was a common culture, a shared discourse that bridged the divisions between theory and practice, reflection and action, arts and science and the other familiar dualities that litter our cultural history.

If there ever was such a culture, it was organised around shared social solidarities rather than common intellectual sympathies. In other words, it was the culture of a narrow predemocratic élite that was doomed either to gradual erosion or revolutionary dissolution. It excluded the experience of women, the working class and non-Europeans and constituted a metropolitan culture that despised provincial and community values, a culture which was often contemptuous of industry, technology and manufacturing (Wiener 1981). Its apparent coherence, its superficial commonality, were more a reflection of its intellectual underdevelopment, of academic amateurism, than of a principled commitment to grand holistic ambitions. As such, it was condemned to obsolescence by the advance of science and the growth of democracy.

The second assumption is the more limited claim that there once existed an organic academic community which has now splintered into uncomprehending fragments. But there is very little evidence, empirical or anecdotal, to support such a claim. If the evolution of higher education, home territory of the most significant segment of the academic community, is considered, an opposite impression is gained. Fifty years ago the gap – social, academic, cultural – between an assistant lecturer at a redbrick university college and an Oxbridge don was far wider than that between their contemporary successors whose lifestyles have tended to converge.

In important ways, higher education is more cohesive than ever, certainly in institutional and professional terms. There is a much stronger sense of the universities, (former) polytechnics and colleges making up a common system with congruent values if not (yet) convergent missions. The promotion of the polytechnics is clear evidence of this. Even further education and adult education are increasingly seen as part of a wider postsecondary education enterprise, a trend that has been strengthened by the incorporation of further education colleges as free-standing institutions independent from local education authorities. They are likely to follow the trajectory travelled by American community colleges a generation ago.

Of course, it can be argued that the establishment of a unified system first of higher education and eventually perhaps of postsecondary education, although producing greater commonality in institutional and professional terms, is likely to have the opposite effect in the normative sphere. The 'old' university, socially secure because of its privileged role in élite formation but academically open because the skills and knowledge it sought to transmit were inherently problematical, nevertheless possessed a firm normative structure. The 'new' university, socially unstable because of mass access but much less open-ended in academic terms, lacks this firm structure. The result of combining such different institutions in a common system is serious value dissonance. A good example is different approaches to assessment. The 'new' university is more likely to adopt a highly structured competencies-based approach, while the 'old' university, because the knowledge in which it trades is often provisional and tentative, will instinctively favour assessment approaches permitting relatively open responses from the students.

A third assumption which is difficult to sustain is that disciplines have drifted further and further apart. A much more prominent, and decisive, feature of modern academic life is the powerful intellectual cross-currents that connect up disciplines. For example, history has been transformed by its more intimate association with the social sciences, notably anthropology. Once a literary-rhetorical discipline, it has acquired more empirical habits, more professionally expressed, and also a taste for theorising. Most disciplines have been transformed by the application of new computer-based technologies which, some believe, provide the basis for an entirely new form of literacy, even of cultural discourse. Certainly these new technologies provide interconnections, technical and intellectual, between disciplines which may bind different branches of knowledge more closely together.

The fourth assumption that must be challenged is that the scientific tradition represents a common stream of rational inquiry, which integrates ideas and experience and so offers an intellectual basis for a liberal discourse-in-common. As has already been argued, there is little in the historical record to support this assumption. It is a disruptive, at times violent, tradition that thrives on intellectual rupture and systematic subversion of established truthes.

The information society: a new democracy?

But there is a further dimension. It has long been recognised that rationality offered an inadequate account of the human condition. A century ago, Nietzsche attacked the false charisma of Reason. Baudelaire wrote as long ago as 1863 of modernity as half 'transient, fleeting, contingent' and half 'eternal and immutable' in a prescient pre-echo of some of the arguments that have swirled round the idea of postmodernism. And Max Weber, of course, realised that the instrumental rationality apparently so triumphant was also an 'iron age' in which the affective, the intimate and the erotic were dully (and dangerously) imprisoned.

Despite all this the image of a stable, ordered liberal civilisation has a powerful hold on the academic imagination. The fear is of an unravelling of that civilisation – of a materialistic, commodified, narcissistic society driven by 'market'/technological imperatives and lacking any moral centre of gravity; and of a centrifugal intellectual system dominated by amoral 'experts' in which any attempt to sustain a common language, never mind a common culture, has been abandoned. But is this an accurate account of the likely shape of a future post-industrial or postmodern society? It is possible that patterns of oppression, or inhibition, typical of industrial society – mass production and enveloping bureaucracy – may simply be replaced by new forms of control: the omnicompetence and omnipresence of advanced information systems will radically reshape the industrial landscape and also our personal lives.

Perhaps this is too gloomy an assumption. In a recent posthumous book Ithiel de Sola Pool, a highly regarded commentator on the cultural significance of new technology, wrote:

> The falling cost of electronic logic supports the trend towards individualization. The growing abundance of band-width in transmission and better management of the electromagnetic spec-

trum creates the technical opportunities for small-group communication. Satellites and fibre links are making costs more distance-
insensitive. (Ithiel de Sola Pool 1990)

Liberals instinctively distrust such technological exuberance. Rightly
so perhaps. They fear new technologies are as likely to produce a new
generation of underpaid outworkers as of free-as-air entrepreneurs,
and under the cloak of consumer choice a deeply conformist commodification of cultural goods. Perhaps these fears are justified.
Advanced information systems in late capitalist societies offer unprecedented opportunities for the individualisation of goods and
services, which in the industrial age had to be mass-provided according to well understood Fordist and Weberian paradigms. But they
also give unprecedented scope for manipulative control, precisely
because they are so pervasive. In a post-industrial society there is
nowhere to hide. Yet, whatever the final judgment, it is wrong to
ignore the immense significance of this knowledge revolution.

Voices of postmodernism

However, it is the contested phenomenon of postmodernism rather
than post-industrialism which is the heart of the debate about the
quality of contemporary academic discourse. It is in this arena that
the forces of fragmentation are most disturbingly encountered. This
is no accident. Postmodernism, to the extent it can be defined at all,
is defined in terms of what it is not. Unlike modernism it does not
make, in the words of Jean-François Lyotard, 'an explicit appeal to
some grand narrative such as the dialects of spirit, the hermeneutics
of meaning, the emancipation of the rational or working subject, or
the creation of wealth' (Lyotard 1984). Into the dustbin of history go
Hegel, Marx, Freud, Adam Smith and other shapers of the modern
world. Instead, according to Lyotard again, postmodernism denies
itself 'the solace of good forms' and seeks 'new presentations not in
order to enjoy them but in order to impart a stronger sense of the
unpresentable.' The obliqueness, opacity even, of this and similar
formulation make it too easy to dismiss postmodernism as merely a
Gallic conundrum. But such a criticism misses the point. The impre-
cision of language which allows meanings to slide past each other
without making proper contact is a central feature of the postmodern
phenomenon.

There is little room in this chapter to speculate about the sources
of postmodernism; the ideological exhaustion of the postwar world
first noted by Daniel Bell more than thirty years ago (Bell 1960) and
powerfully confirmed by the recent collapse of Communism (the last

great metadiscourse descended from the Enlightenment?); the sense
that the firm contours of industrial society were being dissolved by
new technologies; the currents of poststructuralism which emphasised the contingency of meaning and the slipperiness of language;
and a new aestheticism, especially in architecture, which grew out of
a weariness with the restraint and regularity of modernism's classical
forms and also perhaps reflected the shift from 'planning' to 'mar-
kets'. But the eclecticism of, even contradictions between, the various
sources of postmodernism should make us wary of regarding it as a
movement; such a description implies consistency and coherence to
the very characteristics it denies. An excellent account of the evolution of postmodernism has been provided by David Harvey who
weaves together its various strands (Harvey 1989).

The more limited focus of this chapter is on the moral consequences of postmodernism. Has it undermined the idea of culture,
not simply in Arnoldian rhetoric but in routine practice? More seriously for the academic community, has postmodernism discredited
the idea of intellectual integrity, without which an academic community has little purpose? Recently, Jim Collins tried to describe the
postmodern outlook: 'Culture is no longer a unitary, fixed category,
but a decentered, fragmentary assemblage of conflicting voices and
institutions' (Collins 1990). Matthew Arnold no doubt would have
regarded the latter as anarchy rather than culture. We have come a
long way indeed from the Platonic ideal of the good, the true and the
beautiful and even from Arnold's own definition of culture as 'the
fresh and free play of the best thoughts'. Brian Rotman too wrote of
postmodernism's deliberate fragmentation which he admitted its
critics characterised as 'schizophrenic collapse' (Rotman 1990).

The egalitarianism of postmodernism

The prognosis for culture, the idea itself as much as any particular
tradition, appears bleak. Lyotard explicitly denounced what he called
'the nostalgia for the whole and the one', which he regarded as
proto-totalitarian. But two important qualifications must be made.
First, it is not clear that postmodernism has the same fragmentary
effect on individual disciplines. Although it derides grand overarching connections, it may stimulate the creation of a spider's web
of complex interlinks among conventional disciplines. Judged in
postmodern terms, indeed, disciplines comprise the same suspect
metadiscourses which must be ruthlessly deconstructed. And the
effects of this deconstruction and interlinking may be creative. For
example, the study of mentalities in history, which draws on the

insights and techniques of anthropology, psychology and sociology, can be regarded as a typically postmodern enterprise.

Although postmodernism is certainly antiholistic in its grand intentions, it is not party to the reductionist fragmentation of knowledge into increasingly expert disciplines, subdisciplines, specialisms which find it hard to communicate with each other. The latter is a Fordist phenomenon, the development of an ever finer division of academic labour in the cause of improved intellectual productivity. Indeed postmodernism is uneasy with the very idea of expertise. Expertise seems to presuppose the existence of metadiscourses, however low-key, or, at any rate, privileged knowledge into which would-be practitioners must be initiated. It is no accident that the word 'culture' is also applied to professions and disciplines. In postmodern eyes, these professional and academic 'cultures' are as invalid as the grand discourses of Marxism and Freudianism.

Second, it is difficult to regard postmodernism as a true rupture in intellectual life. It merely continues the pattern of modern science. Kuhn's succession of incommensurable paradigms seem to come dangerously close to an endorsement of relativism. Certainly his influence on the social and human sciences has tended to undermine absolutist ideas of rationality. Kuhn's own position has often been misrepresented. When he insisted that Aristotle's, Newton's and Einstein's physics were incommensurable, he did not imply they were of equal scientific validity. His focus was on how and why successive paradigms become established, which he did not believe could be due solely to their superior 'fit' to the empirical evidence but owed a lot to their endorsement by scientific communities.

This touches on a key issue highlighted by postmodernism, the nature of authority which appears to have been abandoned in favour of the delights of difference, a playful diversity. But this is not a new question. Modernity itself was born in the rejection of older patterns of authority, divine or customary. Lyotard himself acknowledged that postmodernism is 'undoubtedly part of the modern'. Anthony Giddens preferred the label 'high modernity' rather than postmodernism to describe the present conjunctures of intellectual life, socio-economic forces and cultural and aesthetic trends. In a recent book he wrote: 'Rather than these developments taking us "beyond modernity", they provide a fuller understanding of the reflexivity inherent in modernity itself' (Giddens 1990).

Longing for order

Three conclusions are possible. First, the idea of a common culture, so nostalgically seductive, is either an aristocratic ideal or a myth, or possibly both. Hard questions, from both democratic and empirical standpoints, must be asked before its alleged unravelling is too effusively deplored. Second, the scientific tradition, rightly, places as high a value on critique as contextualisation; its role is ruthlessly to interrogate those assumptions about the world and our place in it from which we derive comfort and meaning. Radical scepticism is characteristic of both modernism and postmodernism, of liberal civilisation and post-industrial society. Third, our moral restlessness, our worries about the human adequacy of knowledge and skills, are not new. They are at least as old as the industrial revolution and the loss of an assured Christian faith.

This restlessness is not diseased. In a modern industrial society, or a postmodern post-industrial one, it is perfectly healthy. Its absence would be much more alarming. However, this 'liberal conscience' has harmful effects if it is expressed solely in terms of nostalgic regret, which can lead eventually to a rejection of modernity. For example, there is a widespread view that the freedom of higher education has been diminished over the past three decades. The academic community's home territory has been invaded. The golden age of university autonomy has passed. The politicians have crowded in. Accountability, audit, efficiency, effectiveness – these rather than autonomy have become the new watchwords.

The language of nostalgic regret appears to confirm this analysis. But, at best, it is only half true. Historically, it is flawed because it presupposes an earlier state in which universities were significantly more autonomous. This may have been true for a brief quarter century after 1945. But higher education has generally been a creature, as it was a creation, of the state. This analysis is also blind to the very significant academic gains that have accompanied this, arguable, erosion of administrative autonomy. The state has insisted on greater accountability, but mainly because it has made available vastly greater resources. As a result of this massive investment, there are far more student places and much greater opportunities to engage in research than ever before. The life-chances of those who fill these places have been significantly improved. And, despite its frequent reiteration, the awesome extension of intellectual power represented by the apparently trite statistic that half the scientists who ever lived are alive today should never be underestimated.

This is just one example of how the language of liberal longing can mislead. Perhaps contemporary worries about threats to aca-

demic integrity are a distant after-shock of the great clash between
the arts and the sciences, caricatured in the acrimonious debate
between Leavis and C. P. Snow thirty years ago. Perhaps this clash
itself was an after-shock produced by the explosive disengagement
of science from religion a century before. Of course, the world has
changed since the Snow–Leavis conflict. The afterglow of science's
war-time prestige, the object of Leavis' venom, has faded; now concern for the environment and ethical fears about genetic engineering
cast scientists in a more baleful light. The belief in 'the white heat of
the technological revolution', science's immediate and uncontested
role in economic growth, has been superseded by the new emphasis
on business enterprise as the only sure road to wealth creation.

On the other side, humanists have shifted their position. They
have largely abandoned the beleaguered pessimism, and conde-
scension, of the Leavis–Eliot generation. They no longer style themselves guardians of high culture. Indeed many are actively engaged
in deconstructing the very notion of culture as understood by Leavis
and Eliot and, before them, Arnold. They have formed intriguing
alliances with social scientists, but also with computer scientists.
Humanists no longer doubt the relevance of their disciplines to
modern life, a nagging fear that gnawed away at the self-confidence
of an earlier generation. At the time of the Robbins report on higher
education it was assumed that the mass of new students should, and
would, follow courses in science and technology; now the arts and
applied social sciences have become the agents of wider access. So
the rules of engagement in the long war between the arts and the
sciences have been substantially revised.

Truth and meaning

Yet in another form this fissure in intellectual culture continues to
yawn. In the modern intellectual tradition there are really only two
questions that count. First, is it true? – the question asked by Bentham,
Mill, Huxley and their modern descendants, the only one that really
interests working scientists. Second, what does it mean? – the question asked by Coleridge, Arnold and, in perverse ways, Eliot and
Leavis, from which humanists are apt to shrink and which scientists
barely acknowledge. But this duality cannot be regarded necessarily
as a permanent feature of the intellectual landscape. At the outer edge
of physics truth and meaning, observation and interpretation, are
elided. And philosophers, of course, especially those of a postmodern
persuasion, reject both questions as naive. So it is possible to argue
that the dichotomy between truth and meaning will finally be dis-

solved, like older dualities between arts and science, and science and religion.

However, there are two grounds for doubting this outcome. The first is that the truth–meaning dichotomy is deep-rooted, even if it appears in different intellectual disguises. For example, Kuhn's 'normal science' can be aligned with the routine pursuit of truth, research in its usual university sense, while his paradigm shifts can be seen as part of a larger search for meaning, at any rate if meaning is seen as ambitious interpretation. The second is the awkward persistence of ultimate questions about the nature, and therefore purposes, of knowledge. As Weber recognised, rationality fails to address some of the most important, and most personal, aspects of the human condition. And, as Arnold realised half a century before, this bred a sense of dissatisfaction or underfulfillment.

Analytic philosophers generally have followed Hume's rhetorical questions:

> If we take in our hand any volume; of divinity or school metaphysics, for instance; let us ask, Does it contain any abstract reasoning concerning quantity or number? No. Does it contain any experimental reasoning, concerning matter of fact or existence? No. Commit it then to the flames; for it can contain nothing but sophistry and illusion. (Hume 1748)

Their answers, however less brusque than Hume's, have also failed to address the moral restlessness identified by Arnold and Baudelaire, Nietzsche and Weber, a restlessness as central to the western intellectual tradition as the sceptical rationality of the Enlightenment. One virtue of postmodernism perhaps is that it tries to penetrate into the 'sophistry and illusion'.

According to Steiner a more complete understanding, one that helps to soothe this moral restlessness, is to dig down deep into the hidden layers of our intellectual culture. This demands a confrontation with a sense of God or, at any rate, the 'other'. In his recent book, he argued that modern references to God are regarded as echoes of a redundant epistemology, rather as we still refer to sunrise and sunset although we know these phrases offer an inaccurate rendering of the physics of the solar system. As he puts it, 'where God clings to our culture, to our routines of discourses, He is a phantom of grammar, a fossil embedded in the childhood of rational speech.' This he rejects. Reason, knowledge, inquiry, language, meaning are all predicted on the existence of the 'other', whether the shadowy ideals of Plato or the personal God of Christians or Moslems. They are wagers on meaningfulness. We must trust, believe, before we can know.

This is a conclusion which a secular age like our own finds difficult to accept. Like Titus at Jerusalem we gaze on vacant halls and thrones abandoned by their gods. We cannot imagine it otherwise. But paradoxically, the fragmentation of disciplines, the contingency of truth, the slipperiness of language, the characteristics associated (although in different ways) with scientific reductionism and postmodernism, may help to restore a more harmonious balance between reason and faith. Reductionist science and postmodern knowledge no longer aspire to offer absolute overarching truths or to provide authoritative accounts of culture. Liberal civilisation, therefore, will need to ground itself in other values – although not necessarily in Steiner's metaphysics.

References

Bell, D. (1962) *The End of Ideology*. Revised edition. New York: The Free Press.

Bernstein, B. (1971) *Class, Codes and Control*. London: Routledge.

Carlyle, T. (1867) Shooting Niagara: and after? In *Selected Writings* (1971). Harmondsworth: Penguin.

Collins, J. (1989) *Uncommon Cultures: popular culture and post- modernism*. London Routledge.

Eliot, T.S. (1948) *Notes towards a Definition of Culture*. London: Faber.

Giddens, A. (1990) *The Consequences of Modernity*. Cambridge: Polity Press.

Harvey, D. (1989) *The Condition of Postmodernity*. Oxford: Blackwell.

Hume, D. (1748) *An Enquiry concerning Human Understanding*. Oxford: Clarendon Press.

Kuhn, T. (1962) *The Structure of Scientific Revolutions*. Chicago: Chicago University Press.

Leavis, F.R. (1930) *Mass Civilization and Minority Culture*. Cambridge: Cambridge University Press.

Lyotard, J.F. (1984) *The Postmodern Condition*. Manchester: Manchester University Press.

Marx, K. (1965) *The German Ideology*. Marx Engels Selected Works. Moscow.

Popper, K. (1957) *The Poverty of Historicism*. London: Routledge.

Rotman, B. (1990) The Grand Hotel and the shopping mall. *The Times Literary Supplement*, April 6–12, 1990.

de Sola Pool, I. (1985) *Technologies of Freedom*. London: Harvard University Press.

Steiner, G. (1989) *Real Presences*. London: Faber.

Wiener, M. (1981) *English Culture and the Decline of the Industrial Spirit 1830–1980*. Harmondsworth: Penguin.

Chapter 3

Maps of Knowledge
Do They Form an Atlas?

John Wyatt

Introduction

When Adam Sedgwick, the distinguished Cambridge geologist, was writing a set of notes on the geology of the English Lake District to accompany William Wordsworth's *Guide to the Lakes*, he remembered conversations with the poet and praised him for his understanding of the 'universality of nature' (Sedgwick 1842). That phrase marks poet and scientist as members of the significant cultural tradition which a later generation called the Romantic Age. A belief in the essential unity of nature, human nature as well as non-human, for many in that period and for long afterwards into our own times acted as a fundamental, philosophical foundation for understanding the nature of knowledge. Raymond Plant (1974) has explored with considerable clarity the political manifestations of the desire for 'community' since the eighteenth century, but little has been done to delineate the philosophical bases of the notion of community as it was realised in institutions of higher education (see, however,Wyatt 1977, Brubacher 1982). Despite this neglect, the idea persists that knowledge should be, rather than is, interrelated and – a correlation this – that ways of acquiring knowledge or disciplines may be convenient lenses, but may also be selective and even distorting windows into an essentially united reality. I wish to consider the ways in which the idea of universality of knowledge has been discussed and, occasionally, carried into institutional practice.

One aspect of the belief in the unity of formally recognised knowledge which has been strangely neglected in studies of academic cohesion is the relationship between curriculum and institutional form or organisation. Is the university's curriculum a factor for cohesion or are the disciplines within the overall curriculum inherently divided and instinctively disintegrating held together only by the political frame of the university? Is this container, the statutes, ordinances and central services of the university, a bag containing mixed and highly incompatible tricks? The easiest instance in which to see the interrelationship between curriculum and organisation of the institution must be where new institutions are founded or proposed (and they are more often proposed than actually founded). Studies of the inaugural statements of new university chancellors are relatively unexplored areas of study (Wyatt 1990). What follows is an attempt to exemplify some of the patterns of curriculum and organisation from statements either in prospect or in retrospect on the founding of universities.

The University of Berlin of 1809 is a good point to start because it began with a deliberately political act, an explicit manifesto to restore the Prussian nation after the humiliation of defeat by Napoleon. Studies of the origins of the University of Berlin tend to concentrate on the political realism of Wilhelm von Humboldt and, more substantially because he was actually the Rector from 1810 to 1812, of Fichte. Less attention has been given to von Humboldt's ideal curriculum and more to his ideal university structure, which covetous nations, particularly mid-nineteenth century England, wished to emulate in the shape of the professorial system, research quality and departmental units. In fact there was a strong underlying curriculum ideology to the new university. It rested upon von Humboldt's own dream community, the Greek city state. Von Humboldt's Romanticism included a belief in the unbounded universal nature of humanity. It had two dimensions, lateral and contemporary across all existing peoples, but also vertical, in depth, reaching back into a past with which modern Europe shared a common heritage.

Learning was 'an organism, an active force, alive in all its branches and which unites them in each other' (Scott 1960 p.13). The essentially unifying nature of higher learning is seen in von Humboldt's rejection of classification and cataloguing, a rejection not only on academic grounds but also for political reasons – the state loses out!:

> As soon as one stops searching for knowledge, or if one imagines that it need not be creatively sought in the depths of the human spirit but can be assembled by collecting and classifying facts, everything is irrevocably and forever lost for learning which soon vanishes so far out of the picture that it even leaves language like an empty pod and lost for the state as well. (von Humboldt 1963 p.134).

Wholeness is the distinguishing mark of the nature of higher learning. The location of that learning was planned to reflect the Zeitgeist in its search for an ideal, non-repressive community. Associates of von Humboldt and philosophers and writers like Schiller, Fichte,

Schleiermacher, Steffens and Schelling regarded the dual quest for the unity of the outside world of nature and the inner world of humanity as the prime motivator of study. Frequently they used the image of reading the book of Nature, as if, once the language of learning had been discovered, Nature would be opened up to the scholar with its secrets bare. Their writings reveal three key concepts in relating curriculum to institutional identity. First was the notion of a binding discipline, von Humboldt's own binding discipline being the study of the philosophy of language. Second was the idea of a progressive clarification of understanding culminating in an ultimate vision of unity. Third was the idea that there is a hidden, but discoverable, unity in the interconnecting territory between the separate fields of knowledge. The three concepts may be described as keystone structure, ladders of perfection and intersecting spheres. I shall try to exemplify each in a number of different settings where intellectuals have proposed an ideal university.

The keystone

To give an example of a keystone theory I turn, a hundred and thirty years after von Humboldt, to Germany in the 1930s and England in the 1940s. Dismayed by the apparent disintegration of the unity of knowledge, some intellectuals from quite different backgrounds attempted to propose ideal structures of higher education based on the notion of a unifying discipline, a combining factor amongst other disciplines.

In Germany, the Frankfurt Institute, established in 1922 and developed in subsequent years as an independently funded centre for social research, attempted to create a curriculum which brought together the varied social sciences of the Institute, for the purpose of enabling research. Principally under Max Horkheimer, its major director from 1931, a 'keystone' discipline of social philosophy (Sozialphilosophie) was actively encouraged as a stimulus to clarity of vision. Philosophical theory was to interact with as well as reflect on other disciplines, 'a continuing dialectical interpenetration of philosophical theory and the praxis of particular disciplines' (Horkheimer 1931). The enterprise was in fact short-lived because the Institute was politically unacceptable in the 1930s in Germany. At first in Switzerland and then in the United States its members continued their teaching, but in different institutions, with different aims. What must be noted, however, is not the failure of an attempt at unification of knowledge in Frankfurt, but the lasting effects elsewhere of the experiment. Jay notes, 'It was the only interdisciplinary aggregation of scholars working on different problems from a common theoretical base, to coalesce in modern times' (Jay 1973 p.298). The products of the few years of Horkheimer's experiment in curriculum unity are considerable. In the influential work of Adorno, for example, the span of attention across disciplines as diverse as sociology, aesthetics, literary theory and social psychology is a mark of the achievement, based on a theory of binding together by a unifying discipline, that is critical philosophy.

From an experiment which had partial success, I pass to an experiment that never came to fruition. It is from almost the same period, but in its formulation it is more comprehensible. Perhaps its very lucidity accounts for the poor practical outcome, but the proposal deserves consideration because it was driven by some of the same forces that stirred the early Romantics and the 1930s German social scientists to seek unity in a dangerously disintegrating academic culture. F.R. Leavis, of the University of Cambridge's English School, proposed in two works the establishment of a University with the study of literature at its heart. As Horkheimer proposed social philosophy as a critical discipline, a tool to work on and with other tools, so Leavis proposed in *Education and the University* (1943) and in *The Clark Lectures* (1967) that the critical faculties nurtured by a study of literature should act as clarifiers of other subjects. Literature was to be the access to many other disciplines. As Leavis stated in a lecture much later than the publications mentioned above: 'Some day, perhaps, I shall permit myself to brag of the psychologist, the mediaevalist, the anthropologist, the critic of French literature, and so on, distinguished in their respective lives, who once "read English" with me' (Singh 1986 p.181). English was, he claimed, a discipline which trains sensitivity and sensibility. Critical the ideal student may be, but responsive always. Leavis elaborated his proposal with a model curriculum based on a wide-ranging study of the seventeenth century, but the detailed working out of his application need not detain us here, because it did not take place. What it assumed, however, was crucial – a small institution where a key subject would be followed by undergraduate students. Only a small controllable and carefully directed university could conceivably manipulate the student experience through the unifying power of a single discipline. Leavis's scheme is in fact a programme of learning; it lacked an institutional framework to hold that programme together.

The ladder of perfection

What Leavis does exemplify is a much older European tradition, namely faith in aesthetic sensibility, capable of drawing together the diverse and the disparate. Schiller's educational thesis on the *Aesthetic Education of Man* is the classic programme for this ideal of education. First, an appreciation and education in beauty acts as a unifier of the material and the spiritual, of outer and the inner nature: 'By means of beauty, sensuous man is led to forms and thought; by means of beauty spiritual man is brought back to matter and restored to the world of sense' (Schiller 1967 p.123). There is a locking together but also an ascent and a return to ordinary sensation, a keystone and a ladder. In early nineteenth century thought, both in science and in the arts, the idea of a gradually upward, spiritual tendency in values because of education is common. It is present too in conceptions of education by English writers such as Matthew Arnold, T.S. Eliot and F.R. Leavis (see Barnett 1990 ch.7) who saw an influential cultural subject as a preparation for mental and even spiritual attitudes which assist the student on a progressive pathway of learning. The idea of the ascending curriculum, a unity of linked ascent, or a ladder of learning, provides the next set of models for the notion of a community of learning.

Universality, exemplified in the notion of an academic community, or indeed in virtually any setting from the early nineteenth century onwards, hardly ever assumes that there is equality within the commonality of nature. In two senses, there is an implicit hierarchy because humanity is a distinct element within 'nature'. Whatever is assumed about humanity's relationship with the rest of nature, men and women are always the interpreters. There is, undoubtedly, interaction between humanity and the rest of the natural world, but the energy for that interaction is initiated by humanity. Second, the relationship between mankind and nature is almost always an educational one. No matter how attuned the human infant may be to nature, instinctive affinity is only a base for further development. Above that base there is a structure of learning perhaps only leading to a recollection of the golden experience of childhood, but in most cases growing beyond it. The educational process is onwards and upwards in successive stages of sensitivity. In institutional form, that progressive process is incorporated in the conception of the ideal university. In late twentieth century language we could say that Romantic philosophers of higher education have assumed a 'value added', an accumulation of intellectual credit. The highest and most difficult attainment is last in the process of ascending to the heights of knowledge.

The earliest example of a structure relying on the notion of an ascent of learning is much older than the early nineteenth century's flourish of higher education. The mediaeval university of Western Europe took many forms. The curricula varied according to the institutions and the cultures in which they prospered, but a dominant pattern of arts courses provides a model which in changed ways influenced the organisation of university life for centuries. The stepped curriculum of the trivium (grammar, rhetoric, logic) and the quadrivium (music, astronomy, geometry, arithmetic) (Reeves 1969) implied a progression from a wide foundation of study to more complex and demanding specialisms, from preparatory orientation to fulfilment in the study of theology, or medicine or law. This unified ladder of the arts leading up to a socially useful higher learning did not deny that there were different disciplines, but it organised them into a hierarchy, a succession based on a conceptualisation of the nature of knowledge. Underlying the theory of knowledge, there was a pedagogical theory, that people learn effectively through disputation and the arts of language. They become full, useful members of society equipped with techniques of learning as well as with specialist knowledge.

The notion of an ascending order of learning, which is both pedagogically justifiable (at least by common sense and common acceptance) and epistemologically appropriate, is perennial. In the 1960s in United Kingdom during a crucial period of reorganisation of higher education, there was a serious attempt to encourage the building of curricula. The campaign began with an assumption: that the failure of English higher education partly lay in a restrictive form of knowledge, the study of a single academic discipline. A study of the evidence given to the Committee on Higher Education and the Final report itself (the Robbins Report of 1963) reveals a long and fraught argument on the desirability of teaching 'broad' courses. Emerging out of this period of public discussions came not only new courses which attempted to encourage acquisition of ranges of knowledge and corresponding delay in a focus on specialist knowledge, but also, more significantly, new organisations were founded which modelled their undergraduate courses on the assumption of a ladder of learning. Preliminary courses were 'broad', cross-disciplinary and encouraged student choice of new subject areas. Later the components of the course narrowed to the traditional English university first degree of single honours.

The University of Keele is a case in point, where not only was the undergraduate programme built as an initial year's Foundation Course, but, more significantly in institutional terms, the traditional three-year honours degree was extended to four years, so that time could be given to enable undergraduates to develop from this basis (Montford 1972). A fruitful source book for tracing the influence of ideas of the wholeness of knowledge is Scott's biography of Keele's founding Vice-Chancellor, A.D. Lindsay. Included in many revealing statements made at the time of the struggle to found a new university, independent of external London University status, were frequent criticisms of the 'separateness' of the curriculum of the traditional university, and equally frequent and determined efforts to create a cohesive student experience (Scott 1971 p.348).

The new residential universities were not alone in this period in seeking a curriculum-driven attempt to unify the students' experience of higher education, by creating a preliminary period of learning as a basis for later specialisation. The word 'foundation' spread into other higher education institutions. The United Kingdom Open University assumed, on reasonable pedagogic grounds, that part-time students, often of mature age and with work experience, would require preparation before attempting specialist courses. Significantly, the Open University talked of 'levels' above foundation units. There was more than pedagogy in the principles of an ascending curriculum. The foundation subjects were as much about creating a 'new map of knowledge', encouraging explorers to venture into territory which spanned the knowledge spectrum where tastes for further travel along traditional tracks could be nurtured. Teacher training institutions in the United Kingdom in the period of the 1960s also extended the length of their courses on the grounds that education could not be contained in the traditional two-year training courses for non-graduates. Their successfully argued campaign was itself an indication that, for the training college principals, learning was progressive, that processes were ascending as well as cumulative. In the records of these colleges in the 1960s and early 1970s are frequent attempts to create a broad range of studies (often called 'Foundation Courses' or 'Phase One Courses') which deliberately held back the pursuit of a single discipline. These 'monotechnic' institutions were models of a view of learning which was based on the ideal of the college community as a cohesive power, on unity rather than diversity, through a single professional curriculum outcome rather than a collection of subject disciplines.

One example of theory rather than practice, of ideal rather than achievement, shows a very agile mind attempting to unify the curriculum and at the same time to propose a university organisation into which that ideal curriculum fitted. This is Ortega y Gassett's *Mission of the University*, first written in 1930 (translated into English and widely distributed in 1946) in response to a critical political period before the Spanish Civil War. Ortega urged his compatriots to reform the universities on two principles, curricular and pedagogical: what is essential knowledge and how people acquire it. His pedagogical principle was relatively simple: people cannot acquire – with any real sense of taking it into themselves – a great deal of knowledge. Ortega's 'doctrine of parsimony' (Wyatt 1990) is significantly rooted in the period of the Romantic response to the Enlightenment. He quotes Goethe's injunction, 'Free yourself from what is superfluous to yourself' (Ortega 1952). However, the essential core of what remains after discarding the superfluous is a holistic concept of culture. He confidently defines this vast portmanteau term as the 'great cultural disciplines'. These he lists as: the physical scheme of the world (physics), the fundamental thesis of life (biology), the historical processes of the species (history), the structure and functioning of social life (sociology) and the plan of the universe (philosophy). Ortega would create a Faculty of Culture as a nucleus of higher education. In detail, he professed that each of these 'great cultural disciplines' would be covered in succession, leading on to the more complex overview through a study of philosophy. In this example, the unity of knowledge is imposed by extracting from the complex experience of Western culture the essential features of the culture of learning. The student's portfolio would include an allocation in rich but measured quantities of the main aspects of learning, under the control of the university's commitment to 'culture'.

Ortega's ideal university never emerged, but his influence was felt in the United States and in Britain at an important period of planning for universities after the second world war. *Mission of the University* is clearly acknowledged by Lindsay's biographer as a major influence on the foundation of the University of Keele (Scott 1971). At one level, Ortega's scheme reinforced the anxiety of those who gazed with trepidation on the explosion of knowledge. At a different level, Ortega's *Mission of the University* found a prepared, receptive audience for the idea of the university as a bastion against non-cultural forces, the masses. Ortega's broad sweep leads me to the final group of thinkers on the curriculum of higher education who, in different ways, attempted to create an organisation to unify knowledge.

The Venn diagram: 'intersecting spheres'

The intersecting circles of a Venn diagram create the appropriate image for the next type of university builder, as the rungs of a ladder or a keystone have been for my other two groups. If each circle represents a traditional discipline or subject, then where one circle overlaps with another there is a fruitful sector of learning. It is at the boundaries and, above all, in the touching, intersecting boundaries of knowledge that new insights are gained. This category of thinkers about the university and its curriculum, in contrast to Ortega, accepted the diversity and diffusion of forms of knowledge. Indeed, some argued that to claim the universality of knowledge necessarily implied constant change and reform, because nature was always in flux. They accepted growth and change, fission and branching, tracks in knowledge. J.H. Newman's seminal *The Idea of a University*, though praised continuously as a defence of a 'liberal education', is, on close examination, a passionate argument for the university being judged by a fundamental criterion, that it teaches the whole conspectus of knowledge (not, of course, practical and vocational knowledge). Newman's defence of the place of theology in any university, as well as in the new Catholic University of Dublin, is at bottom an argument that all human knowledge must be represented and that theology would be a ghost at the feast if it were not there. Because Newman sees unity from a divine external source, he can justify an inclusive curriculum and an organisation which embraces all learning: 'I have said all branches of knowledge are connected together because the subject matter of knowledge is intimately united in itself, as being the acts and work of the Creator' (Newman 1873 p.127).

What more is there to say, other than that in the quest for universality, the university should contain all human aspiration to knowledge? If that principle were all, then the simple organisational proposition would be 'the bigger the better.' Mega-knowledge produces mega-divisions of knowledge, and thence mega-university. 'Polytechnic' begins to emerge out of a mist of definition as a justifiable curricular title. In practice, however, in the 1960s, rejecting simplistic theories of growth, those who pursued the quest for unity in the kingdom of knowledge turned attention to the interstices of the divisions of knowledge, hence my image of the Venn diagram. A quest for interdisciplinarity has led to a number of experiments and a number of proposals for 'relatedness' as the foundation of a university system.

A 'locus classicus' is another document produced like Ortega's out of war and collapse of the state. Karl Jaspers' *Idea of the University*, was published after the Second World War and, again like Ortega's work, translated and read at a time of university reform in the United Kingdom and the United States. Jaspers' text is a concentrated argument. A full understanding of his educational thesis requires a reading of his more substantial philosophical works, so I can do no justice to the proposals he makes for an ideal university. I shall instead identify a core position, which is best put by Jaspers himself:

Whatever exists in the world should be brought into the scope of the University so as to become the object for study... [The former member of the university engaged in] a living exchange with the scholarly community to which some day he may return. (Jaspers 1960 pp.56 and 57)

The mission may be universal and expansive in curricular terms, but it is also centripetal, concerned with exchange within the curriculum. Jaspers' key to intellectual development is in the contact between disciplines. It is in the borders of learning where one discipline meets another that research goes on (should go on?), and where humanity finds its true excitement and renewal.

The notion of planning for 'exchange' between disciplines was most clearly taken up in the United Kingdom in the founding of a unique university in the 1960s. The University of Sussex was established with the intention of solving virtually the same problems as the University of Keele (the expansion of student numbers, the need to unify the student experience), but took an essentially different approach (see Daiches 1964). The words of one of the founding members written in a retrospective essay after twenty-five years explains the key attitude: 'Suffice it to say here that our undergraduate courses and academic organisation should provide for the full exploitation of interdisciplinary studies. Hence the formulating of Schools of Studies rather than Departments, and the commitment to "Contextual Studies" on the Arts and Social Studies side of the University and to the Major/Minor degree structure on the Science side'. The reminiscence adds that many 'yearned from time to time' for the cosiness, tidiness and relative simplicity of departmental structure', although the Sussex system has 'stood the test of time' (Blin-Stoyle and Ivey 1986 p.xiv). The fascinating accounts by Daiches (1964) and by Briggs (1986) reveal not only a commitment to innovation in cross-disciplinary work, but also a deliberate decision to teach in a distinctive way. At first, standard teaching loads for all members of a faculty, including professors, were based on an allocation of tutorials. Traditional lectures, if they were to be given, were not to be included in the load, because of a pedagogic ideal of teaching by something close to the Socratic method. Interesting phrases are prominent in the text quoted above such as 'founding fathers', 'style and ethos', 'elan' (rather than 'morale'), and particularly the perennial phrase, 'The Sussex Map of Learning' (Briggs 1986 p.9). The notion of interdisciplinality does not merely assume the accumulation by a student of more than one discipline. In the minds of the planners and idealists at least, if not in the minds of the learner, a new territory of knowledge is created by the deliberate act of interrelating disciplines.

Phrases such as 'working on the boundaries' between areas of knowledge, 'creating new maps of learning/knowledge' intimate something more profound than regrouping departmental structures. Those who have visions of the essential unity of knowledge are professing a new way of experience. The university could become, in their view, a new kind of colony devoted to human growth. It is rare to find a rhetoric which says, 'university studies enable us to see the world the way people outside our walls see it.' Rather the argument runs, 'university studies enable us to see the world as it really is, a united undivided whole.' This thesis suggests a progressive and clarifying role for learning. These reformers were doubly visionary because they proposed a reform of learning engendering a reform of teaching.

Is the quest for universality over?

I have attempted to describe a few models of the application of the ideal of the universality of knowledge to curriculum, real or wished for, and, where it was attempted, to the organisation of the institution that assisted the delivery of the curriculum. How far can the modern university continue to explore aspirations of wholeness? My conclusion is that at the level of the whole university the notion of wholeness or universality of knowledge is not likely to succeed. However, at a lower level, within a department or division, academic planning may enable cohesion, unity of learning or interdisciplinarity to take place.

In the last decade of the century, the forces at work in the creation of new universities, or the re-formation of older institutions, are formidable and, at root, from a very different philosophical tradition than the influences that sought integration of the curriculum. Some of these disintegrating forces are explored elsewhere in this volume. Inevitably, a strong philosophical strand is rational-materialism. Institutions are constructed on the analogy of the industrial product, the commercial market and the factory machine-driven process. There are more recent philosophical origins. Utilitarianism is still alive and well in the reconstruction of institutions planned for the greatest good of the greatest number. The 'outside community' permits the university to exist for a general good; it pays for as well as benefits from higher education. The modular curriculum is a peculiar modern version of utilitarian economics. The range of goods on offer is open for free choice. 'Consumers' in universities, like consumers in the streets, will choose what gives most pleasure and least long-term pain, which in the best social circumstances will encourage a market system which works by self-interest. On the one hand, a modularised degree with open choice of areas of study is making a statement about the nature of knowledge and about the equality of disciplines. If every item is equal, then the learner – not the teacher – is the person who connects aspects of learning. In fact, modularisation is not a proposition based on wholeness of knowledge, but on a principle of the equality of all aspects of knowledge. It is about choices not about connections. Postmodernist echoes are apparent!

Moving from philosophical backgrounds to practical fore-grounds, the development of new universities in the last twenty years could not be described in any way as the creation of *new* 'centres' of learning, if 'centre' implies cohesion. Accretion is a much more appropriate word. Size, and that much abused metaphor prevalent in the 1980s in the United Kingdom, 'critical mass', become crucial. A sufficient spread of disciplines to maintain a large enough base is the chief criterion of a well-founded university with 'large enough' being economically, not academically, defined. In fact, the main cri-terion for inclusion of a subject in a university curriculum is no longer what former generations would have pursued, the appropriateness of the subject in the family of learning. It is to do at one level with the subject's social usefulness, at another level for individual students of universities, more crudely, 'will it pay?' or 'will it avoid making a loss for the university?'

There are other conditioning factors. Some university organisa-tions have grown in the same way that industrial organisations grow, by merger and other forms of inclusion. As well as relying on a simple axiom, 'greater is better', there is often a statement of the value to the merged or incorporated element of joining an established reputable organisation. This rationale for merger is common where small pro-fessional schools or colleges (monotechnics) are subsumed into a larger (polytechnic) organisation. In the United Kingdom, the pre-vious patterns of small professional institutions, often teaching at a lower level of higher education, with little research base, have be-come the exception rather than the rule. Nursing education, teacher training, social work education and health-related professions, for example, merge with a university to form a school (or a department in a school). These organisational structures make, of course, curricu-lar statements as well as structural adjustments. The practical disci-pline is admitted to the universe of knowledge defined by the host body's curricular structure. Indeed, there is a claimed value for the association of disciplines with other disciplines. 'Claimed' because there is little evidence of a reform of structures to encourage interdisciplinarity. In most instances, the new unit is tacked onto or lost within the old.

A good illustration of the curricular philosophy of the late twentieth century is provided by the organisation for the disbursement of funds from a sequence of government agencies in the United Kingdom since 1985. In order to make comparisons between institutions, colleges and universities are obliged to render returns on student and staff numbers. These have to be arranged according to very traditional curricular patterns. Subject groupings in these returns are of cognate disciplines. The fact that a student's experience may be across a range of disciplines, or that some courses exist 'between' disciplines, is an untidy aspect, which does not fit the questions asked by the funding council. The concept of knowledge underlying this bureaucratic system is one of common discipline titles grouped into broad or cognate categories. Although there is no direct guidance to individual institutions, the presumption is that the information gathering aspect of the organisation is similarly organised. This procedure is a reinforcement of the traditional Faculty and Departmental academic structure. It is a collection system not a cohesion.

A bureaucratically generated system linked to funding and resourcing is a powerful force for the disintegration of the notion of the universality of knowledge. In a collection system there is an inbuilt requirement to relate to institutional structures outside the university. The purpose of the data gathering is to compare subjects not within university A or university B but between university A and university B. The curriculum has, in its final stages as collected data, become national. Simultaneously, other externalising agencies are at work. The student on a credit-accumulating degree for instance has become nationally educated, for he or she could truthfully be said to study literature or science at the University of Anywhere in the UK.

What remains of the tradition of universality of knowledge in the face of these powerful institutionalised and nationalised developments? One response is to locate the remnants of the idea of unity elsewhere than in the curriculum. The organisation itself provides a centre for unifying principles in its affectively oriented suborganisations, such as students unions, student welfare systems, pastoral organisations. The outward and visible signs of unity are symbols of identity such as logos, fraternity pins, badges and sports teams strips, newsletters, and publicity material. These are very clear explicit responses to a search for a sense of community. It should not be forgotten that there is an honourable ancestry. One of Newman's most famous passages about the ideal university puts its emphasis on the non-instrumental components of a student's life:

It will give birth to a living tradition, which in course of time will take the shape of a self-perpetuating tradition, or a *genius loci*, as it is sometimes called, which haunts the home where it has been born, and which imbues and forms, more or less, and one by one, every individual who is successively brought under its shadow. (Newman 1873 p.167)

There the situation could be left, with the long tradition of sense of academic community almost dead or at least in pseudo form masquerading as a public relations exercise. I believe however that there is still an opportunity to extract from the experience of the last two hundred years of learning a vision of the interconnected nature of knowledge in higher education. The problem is to distinguish that vision from vague backward glances to idealised communities of learning or from anti-intellectual feelings or from holistic solutions to crises of disintegration. When Europe attended to the centenary celebrations of the French Revolution, we had to do more than cry, 'Good ideals, pity about the heads in the baskets!' Similarly we must re-examine with care what ideals of value remain from the 'academic Romantic Revolution'. One is the vitality of scholarship at the connecting points between disciplines. Jaspers calls these sectors, 'grenzensituationen' or boundary situations. Second, dialogue was always an essential feature of von Humboldt's scheme for a university, and it was an essential virtue, more than a pedagogical device, in later formulations of ideal universities from Newman onwards. Third is the ideal of a universality of knowledge. This last ideal is perhaps hardest of all for the English universities, which from the mid-nineteenth century onwards, not only in higher education, but also in school systems which feed the universities, have seen specialism and single disciplinary concentration as the mark of academic excellence. However, there are now considerable opportunities for students to select pathways to a first degree which are not specialised and 'narrow', to use the jargon of the Robbins Report. The danger is that these selections may be incoherent in relation to each other, with no ambition to unify the student experience. The challenge is now to design maps which make sense for those who pursue knowledge through its diverse forms and distinctive disciplinary approaches.

One familiar aspect of the age which later generations called the Romantic Revolution is the focus on self-reflection. A positive habit we can learn from this ideal of inward exploration is, to use the favourite metaphor of thinkers on the nature of knowledge, to make maps, but maps which are not private devices. If there are to be exchanges between scholars and teachers in different disciplines, and not competitive squabbling for grants and research funds, then attention will be required for the difficult task of explaining to each other what each has set out do and what distinctive methods have been employed. Communication is one of the transferable skills to which we pay lip service in higher education. 'The chattering classes' is a slur used by people of action. It may be that the universities should chatter more internally as well as externally, and engage in less action.

References

Barnett, R. (1990) *The Idea of Higher Education*. Buckingham: Open University Press/SRHE.

Blin-Stoyle, R. and Ivey, G. (eds) (1986) *The Sussex Opportunity*. Brighton: Harvester.

Briggs, A. (1986) The Years of Plenty, 1961–1976. In R. Blin-Stoyle and G. Ivey (eds) *The Sussex Opportunity*. Brighton: Harvester. pp.1–21.

Brubacher, J.S. (1982) *On the Philosophy of Higher Education*. San Francisco: Jossey Bass.

Daiches, D. (ed) (1964) *The Idea of a New University*. London: Deutsch.

Horkheimer, M. (1931) Die gegenwartige lage der sozialphilosophie. In *Frankfurter Universitatsreden*, xxxvii.

Humboldt, W. von (1963) *Humanist without Portfolio*. (trans. M. Cowan. Detroit: Wayne State U.P.)

Jaspers, K. (1960) *The Idea of the University*. London: Owen.

Jay, M. (1973) *The Dialectical Imagination*. London: Heinemann.

Leavis, F.R. (1943) *Education and the University*. Cambridge: CUP.

Mountford, J. (1972) *Keele, an Historical Critique*. London: RKP.

Newman, J.H. (1873) *The Idea of a University*. Oxford: Clarendon.

Ortega y Gassett, J. (1952) *Mission of the University*. London: RKP.

Plant, R. (1974) *Community and Ideology*. London: Routledge and Kegan Paul.

Reeves, M. (1969) The European university from mediaeval times. In W.R. Niblett (ed) *Higher Education: Demand and Response. London: Tavistock.*

Robbins, Lord (1963) *Higher Education*. London: HMSO.

Schiller, F. (1967) *On the Aesthetic Education of Man*. Oxford: Clarendon.

Scott, D. (1971) *A.D. Lindsay: A Biography*. Oxford: Blackwell.

Scott, D.F.S. (1960) *William von Humboldt and the Idea of a University*. University of Durham inaugural lecture.

Sedgwick, A. (1842) Three letters upon the geology of the Lake District. In Hudson and Nicholson (ed) *A Complete Guide to the Lakes*. London: Longman.

Singh, G. (ed) (1986) *F.R. Leavis: Valuations in Criticisms and other Essays*. Cambridge: CUP.

Wyatt, J.F. (1977) The idea of community in institutions of higher education. *Studies in Higher Education 2*, No.2.

Wyatt, J.F. (1990) *Commitment to Higher Education*. Buckingham: Open University Press/SRHE.

Part II

Community Through Academic Inquiry

Chapter 4

Interdisciplinarity and Community

Tony Becher

The unity of knowledge

One aspect of the quest for unity within the academic world lies in the concern for a greater sense of intellectual coherence. Those who argue for the closer unification of knowledge, or against its progressive fragmentation, do so for a number of different reasons. It is perhaps significant that even the unitarians are not fully united in their justification of their common cause. One argument stems from a predominantly social motive: the academic community is damagingly divided, and only an improvement in the level of mutual communication and understanding can ameliorate the progressive onset of chaotic sectarianism. Another approach is philosophical in its emphasis, pointing to the apparently incoherent and fragmentary nature of what we regard as established knowledge rather than to defects among the knowers. The issue might from this standpoint be described as one of converting a patchwork quilt into a seamless cloak. Then there are those whose anxieties are neither social nor philosophical, but utilitarian. Many of today's most pressing concerns, it is contended, cannot be adequately tackled from the vantage point of any single discipline: what is needed is an interdisciplinary strategy which overrides, and indeed renders obsolete, the conventional disciplinary divisions. My subsequent comments will take some account of each of these perspectives, but the main emphasis will be on the first, socially-derived rationale for promoting greater harmony among the disparate groups engaged in the pursuit and transmission of knowledge.

It is a sound injunction that those who comment on value-laden issues should not pretend to neutrality, but should make it manifest where they themselves stand. My attitude towards the quest for a common academic culture can best be explained by reference to a classic contribution to political theory: namely, Charles Lindblom's seminal article on *The Science of Muddling Through* (Lindblom 1959). In it, he contrasts two fundamentally different approaches to the resolution of policy problems, which he labels respectively the root method and the branch method. The first of these is appropriately radical, but at the same time imbued with a strong sense of rationality. It depends on starting with a clean slate, clarifying and crystallising the objectives of the policy in question, investigating all the feasible means of achieving those objectives, systematically evaluating the relative effectiveness of each approach, and adopting the one calculated to have the highest probability of success. The second, branch method is more modest in its ambitions. It involves acceptance rather than dismissal of the *status quo*, and calls for no more than a series of small steps moving from it towards a broadly defined goal, each step constituting a successive approximation to a state of affairs whose conception may itself be subject to negotiation and modification as the iteration proceeds.

Admirers of Karl Popper may discern in Lindblom's branch method something akin to the 'piecemeal social engineering' advocated in *The Open Society and its Enemies* (Popper 1966). It is this piecemeal approach that I favour, in relation to the achievement of intellectual unity as well as to other, even more major, issues such as the distribution of world resources and environmental preservation. Put starkly, the choice of strategies for tackling the issue lies between strongly partisan proselytising and attempts at mass conversion on the one hand – designed to bring about a revolutionary shift in attitudes – and a more limited but equally determined strategy of what Lindblom labelled 'disjointed incrementalism'. To opt for the one approach rather than the other is, I suspect, more a matter of personal temperament than of superior intellect or greater natural virtue.

In the end, the two may indeed turn out to complement each other. The incrementalist approach can come to nothing if it fails at the last to change basic structures and assumptions. The move towards universal suffrage has had in most political systems the jerky, erratic progress characteristic of Lindblom's branch method, but has culminated in major change. One might thus argue that successful incrementalism has eventually to lead to radical reform. But on the other side, revolutionary slogans are not enough on their own: they have to connect with slow, piecemeal changes in people's everyday lives. It may take a zealot to begin the difficult business of changing entrenched habit and opinion (as in the case of the recent campaigns against smoking or drink driving), but the necessary amendments in house rules or legislation and policing call for a less dramatic, more low-key process of incremental evolution. And that is to suggest that proselytising is only effective if it yields in the end to gradual but fundamental adjustment. Either way, major shifts in attitude and belief take time; and reformers may choose, according to temperament, whether to buy that time at the beginning or at the end.

It may be inferred from what has been said that my attitude towards the unification of academic activity is sympathetic, but agnostic. There are many difficulties in the way of halting the fragmentation which already exists in the scholarly community. It is – at least from an incrementalist's perspective – important to recognise, as realistically as one can, what those difficulties comprise. They may be divided into those which are unlikely to yield to pressure or persuasion, and those which – though stubborn to remove – might succumb to a well-planned programme of reform. It will be useful to consider the former, intractable problems first.

One possible entry into the exploration of the issues is to ask why knowledge is organised in the way it is. There are three well-known answers to that question, each unfortunately incompatible with the other two. Each of them has, moreover, very different implications for would-be reformers. The first, which is usually labelled the realist position, holds to the simple view that the state of human knowledge directly reflects the nature of reality. To put it in a fancy slogan, epistemology mirrors ontology. If that were indeed held to be the case, there could be no more to be done. To try to change the configuration of knowledge could not affect the underlying given, the world as it is: the only outcome would be to detach knowledge from reality, and hence to degrade it into mere illusion.

Many of us, however, tend nowadays to adopt a more sophisticated view, leaving 'naive realism' as the fading empire of a few old-fashioned professional philosophers. It is the sociologists and anthropologists who have above all made relativism respectable, with their insistent suggestions that knowledge is 'socially constructed'. We view the world as we do, according to this contention, because we have been indoctrinated by our own cultural milieu. What we see is a product of our collective and individual histories. Where different people perceive the same things differently, it is not a matter of one being right and the other wrong, since 'right' and 'wrong' have no meaning independent of the context in which they are used. On this thesis, the current configuration of academic knowledge is a result of mere historical accident: had history been otherwise, there might have been no mathematics, no chemistry, no history to be otherwise, and perhaps no social science to tell us that realism is an illusion. The reformer's task is accordingly relatively simple: it is merely to change the course of future events by changing the cultural norms. Once disciplines are clearly seen to be the products of no more than prejudice and habit, their hegemony can be challenged. A new world view can be promulgated which will eventually do away with the artificial divisions which currently ensnare us and drive us apart.

The third account of the nature and status of human knowledge is frankly pragmatic. Some might more dismissively describe it as functionalist. Knowledge fields, on this view, are as they are because they happen to work. Physics survives as an organised discipline, and physicists as a clearly identifiable community, because there happens to be a whole range of interrelated questions which are amenable to its associated investigative techniques. The status of geography is less certain, because it seems to be a subject without a clearly- defined centre. Economics has prospered since the days of its founding fathers, but its current credibility has diminished with successive failures of prediction. Reform of the structure of knowledge must depend on identifying more useful ways of organising human enquiry; and insofar as the solution is held to lie in interdisciplinary investigation, that too must justify itself in operational terms.

Constraints on interdisciplinary enquiry

The concept of interdisciplinarity, like other concepts related to the academic domain, has two distinct aspects: the social and the cognitive. To be aware of the constraints in the way of its promotion, it is necessary to look at the social and cognitive features of knowledge communities, and to remind ourselves of how they operate.

Starting first with the social dimension, it has to be recognised that specialisation imposes what Ruscio (1985) described as an 'iron law'. It is the inexorable result of every go-getting academic's need to compete for scholarly reputation with others in the same field. Typically, this will lead to attempts to establish and colonise a particular patch in which one's own special expertise can be demonstrated. Often that patch will be narrowly bounded and deeply penetrated. Pre-eminence – with important exceptions – is not seen to derive from broad (and certainly not from shallow) subject-matter coverage. For many academics, asking them to abandon their closely-contained specialisms and to widen their frames of reference is akin to urging the citizenry to suspend their strong local loyalties, abandon their sense of nationhood, and see themselves as members of a wider and more diverse multinational community. It can be done – and is perhaps happening, very slowly, in relation to the UK's membership of the EU – but it is a precarious and protracted affair, allowing of sudden reversions to nationalism and the slow business of acclimatising a new generation more readily than the old. One example of how that acclimatisation may come about in the academic context relates to the post-war unification and quantification of the biological sciences, in which the earlier specialisms, based mainly on taxonomic distinctions, began to give way to an approach focusing on general mechanisms and processes. The Old Guard failed for the most part to make the adjustment. Doing so was left to the Young Turks, aided by an immigrant cohort of physicists moving into what they saw as a challenging new arena (Mulkay 1974).

What can the reformers offer as the rewards for heeding their injunctions? Interdisciplinary work cannot by any means guarantee – though it can on occasion promote – more original and fruitful research or a better professional reputation than specialised mono-disciplinary enquiry. It may hold out a promise of a better collective defence against a hostile environment, on the 'united we stand, divided we fall' principle. It may also be argued to demonstrate a stronger sense of accountability and a clearer acceptance of social responsibility, in that its concern is often with pressing problems which do not seem amenable to monodisciplinary solutions. But such lofty aims are rather remote from the everyday concerns and the understandable career ambitions of most academics. Even where some commitment to interdisciplinary activity exists, the problems of achieving coherence among a diversely-trained team of people remain. A clinical psychologist specialising in child abuse commented to me recently how difficult it was to reconcile her own emphasis on the interests of the individual child with the social worker's concern for the restoration of family relationships and the prime motivation of the police to obtain a successful prosecution: yet all three groups were expected to operate as a coherent team in their attempts to resolve any particular case. In a somewhat similar vein, a sociologist of science (Pinch 1990) recently wrote of an experiment in solar-neutrino physics, involving nuclear physicists, astrophysicists, neutrino-physicists and radio-chemists. When the experiment went wrong, he noted that 'scientists from each discipline (*sic*) would perceive one or more of the other disciplines as being the cause of the problem... when it came to their own discipline, expressions of confidence were often made.'

It may, then, be a difficult social process to build up a coherent and coordinated group of people working on the interface of two or more different disciplines. In my study of disciplinary cultures, I came across one such group, in the field of space physics, comprising physicists, chemists, an engineer and a computer scientist. The leader of the group, after assuring me how effectively they had learned to work together, confessed himself to be in despair. The computer scientist was leaving shortly for a better-paid and more senior post; there was no-one to be found with an appropriate background to replace him, and the team was faced with the slow process of inducting a newcomer to their particular way of working and thinking. This example reminds us, not only how unified interdisciplinary activity is itself difficult to bring about, but also how even here, highly specialised knowledge may be at a premium.

The issues noted so far – the more evident rewards of specialisation, the problems of ingrained disciplinary loyalties and the need for time to build up a working interdisciplinary team – are predominantly social in their origins and emphasis. But there are cognitive issues to be considered as well. It is undeniable that an individual academic who is able in his or her person to combine two or more sets of disciplinary skills may succeed in coming up with important and original findings. One of the many examples of this process is Joseph Needham, who has been able to combine his expertise as a biochemist and his capabilities as a sinologist to produce his monumental study *Science and Civilization in China* (Needham 1956–1988).

The rare combination of abilities needed to undertake such achievements is however itself a reminder of one important cognitive feature of interdisciplinarity. Needham's could fairly be described as a one-off intellectual triumph: his research has generated no obvious line of academic succession, no latterday disciples dedicated to continuing and extending his work. To say this is not to imply that Needham's *magnum opus* will have no long-term impact on scholarship. It will doubtless remain for many years a key reference source for both sinologists and historians of science, and may well provide a starting point for other scholarly activity. But the particular combination of skills that the work required is unlikely to be widely replicated, and insofar as the investigation is taken forward it is likely to be in a piecemeal fashion uncharacteristic of a fully-fledged intellectual tradition. Those who are dubious about the significance of interdisciplinary enquiry are prone to point critically to this feature of its apparent lack of continuity. In common with the hybrid mule, the hybrid research topic seems regrettably incapable of reproducing itself.

To make matters worse, where such an accusation can be shown to be invalid – where a combined attack on a problem from two or more different disciplinary perspectives proves to be particularly fruitful – the result is no more favourable to the advocates of interdisciplinarity. Once it becomes evident that a wide new arena has been opened up for subsequent exploration, a new kind of specialism begins to establish itself, gradually acquiring all the features of a conventional academic discipline in its own right. This is precisely what happened in the cases of biochemistry and biophysics: and it is what now seems to be happening in the field of cognitive sciences, defined by one leading exponent as covering 'psychology, logic, linguistics, artificial intelligence, and neuroscience (and, potentially, anthropology). More accurately, it covers *a particular approach* [author's emphasis] to these subjects, whereby they are seen as integral parts of an interdisciplinary research programme into the nature of mind' (Boden 1991). The 'particular approach' is already being embodied in a new series of degree programmes, a collection of dedicated journals, a special library classification, one or more professional associations, and all the other trappings of a standard disciplinary community.

To sharpen, simplify and polarise the argument, it would seem that interdisciplinary activity is in cognitive terms a loser almost by definition. If it deals effectively with a particular issue, but fails to generate further research, it is branded as sterile. If it is successful in giving rise to a rich and productive line of enquiry, that enquiry is prone to be labelled as a new discipline, and hence as no longer a valid example of interdisciplinarity.

Cognitive considerations

The considerations so far advanced point to a generally pessimistic conclusion. Cognitively, as well as socially, there would seem to be quite daunting barriers in the way of achieving a greater degree of intellectual coherence in the academic world. Nonetheless, it is necessary to remind ourselves that there are more positive features, suggesting the possibility of at least some modest, incremental moves in the direction the unitarians would wish to go.

In the first place, disciplines themselves are far from being monolithic. While they might seem to be set in concrete from the macro perspective which tends to be adopted by an outsider, seen from an inside, micro perspective they appear, rather, to be in a constant Heraclitean state of flux. Bucher and Strauss (1961), in their study of medical specialisation, underline the heterogeneity of the various groupings and the divergence of interests between them, writing of 'loose amalgamations of segments pursuing different objectives in different manners and more or less delicately held together under a common name at a particular period in history.' Every discipline has its constituent specialisms, and many of these are in turn subdivided (so that Mulkay 1977, for example, was able to refer to a classification of solid state physics into 'twenty-seven relatively distinct fields of investigation').

Such subdisciplinary elements can be represented as forming a counter-culture to that of their parent disciplines, in that they may generate overlaps of interest between specialist groups in neighbouring knowledge domains (Becher 1990). These overlaps are manifested in various ways: through boundary disputes between one discipline and another; through a process of boundary maintenance, involving an explicit or tacit division of intellectual labour; or sometimes through a sense of close identification between the inhabitants of the territories concerned. Pinch (1990) comments that 'Although... I may call myself a sociologist and introduce my colleague from the next office as a sociologist, my own research on the rhetoric of science has more in common with linguists working at other universities than with the person in the next office.' Buchanan (1966) argues that 'it is easier for an economist working with non-market decisions to communicate with a positive political scientist, game theorist or organisational psychology theorist than it is for him to communicate with a growth-model macro-economist with whom he scarcely finds any common ground.' Similarly, one of the mechanical engineers interviewed in my study of disciplinary cultures (Becher 1989) claimed to have more in common with mathematicians studying fluid mechanics than with other engineers studying his own research topic of combustion.

These considerations hold out the prospect of a limited but nonetheless significant series of linkages between different knowledge fields at the subdisciplinary level. In his own persuasive advocacy of the unification of the social sciences, Campbell (1969) urged the development of 'collective comprehensiveness through overlapping patterns of unique narrowness', and the creation of 'a continuous texture of narrow specialties which overlap other specialties', as against 'trying to fill these gaps by training scholars who have mastered two or more disciplines.' He saw this as calling for a 'fish scale model' in which specialist research areas overlap like the scales on a fish, so bringing about 'a collective communication, a collective competence and breadth.' One is reminded of Wittgenstein's (1953) metaphor of a rope, which derives both its unity and its resilience not from a continuous thread of material running through its length but from a great multiplicity of short, overlapping fibres.

It is also important to recognise the tendency all of us have to fall back on a simple stereotype of an academic discipline, much as we are liable to conjure up a too-ready notion of research. One has only to look at some of the recent policy decisions of the governmental agencies responsible for funding higher education in the UK – and they at least ought to know better – in relation to research selectivity, financing and planning, for it to be obvious that they are dominated by the vision of elaborate equipment, large teams and substantial budgets. Yet even in the sciences, most research groupings are relatively small, do not depend on vast apparatus and make only limited financial demands; while in the humanities and social sciences, which account for the majority of academic staff, research is largely individual and costs very little more than the time of the people engaged in it. This does not prevent academic policy-makers from behaving as if the academic world were engaged predominantly in the study of high energy particle physics, space science and radio astronomy.

There is, in a similarly misleading way, an inclination to speak as if everyone in academia can be identified as belonging to an established disciplinary grouping, modelled on the tidy prototypes of history in the humanities, economics in the social sciences and physics among the sciences. In actuality, there are a number of areas of enquiry centred on a particular theme, but not identified with a particular intellectual approach: many of them carry the tell-tale label of 'studies' – European studies, women's studies, media studies and the like. From a conventional academic perspective, some of them – black studies is a case in point – might be dismissed as intellectually dubious and organisationally unstable. In cognitive terms, their validity depends on holistic and pragmatic arguments (Klein 1990); in social terms, it is manifested by their continued survival in the face of sustained hostility, and by the steady increase in their range of coverage and the numbers of their adherents.

It is even more surprising that arguments about interdisciplinarity tend to overlook the existence of the very large category of academic subjects which deal with practical concerns, including medicine, architecture, engineering, social work and education. The training for most such professional areas draws, *inter alia*, on a number of different academic disciplines: medicine on various of the biological sciences, statistics and demography; architecture on aesthetics and materials science; engineering on management as well as on mathematics and the physical sciences; social administration on political science and sociology; education on psychology, sociology and other areas of social science. Whether one chooses to label them as interdisciplinary, or merely as applied or professional subjects, they are clearly very different in kind from the traditional disciplines, both in their shared concern with vocational preparation and in their generally heterogeneous and eclectic knowledge.

Social considerations

But the concerns that lie behind the debate about the fragmentation of knowledge commonly go deeper than this. The mere fact that different disciplines can be brought to bear on particular kinds of problems in no way ensures that the proponents of those several disciplines enjoy a common set of interests and values, a mutual sense of respect and a shared tolerance of each others' idiosyncrasies. What is needed, it may be argued, is something more fundamental than an overlap of specialisms or a combination of intellectual perspectives. The real problem lies in people's attitudes rather than their practices; and its solution must be found in a way of changing those attitudes in the direction of promoting a sense of intellectual commonality.

This brings us back to the view earlier identified, of academic unity as a predominantly social issue. Seen in these terms, the situation is not as drastic as the pessimists would lead us to suppose. There are a number of promising trends worth reviewing. One relates to the apparent convergence of values and practices in different areas of knowledge. A well-informed observer of the academic scene, the American anthropologist Clifford Geertz (1980), saw signs as long as a decade ago of a 'culture shift', a 'refiguration of social thought' bringing the humanities and the social sciences closer together in their intellectual kinship, as the latter moved away from 'physical process analogies to symbolic form ones'. It does indeed seem the case that historians and sociologists are wandering more freely nowadays into each others' territories, even if important differences of method and approach remain. But it also has to be remarked that any coming-together of this kind is likely to be at the expense of the previously dominant scientific paradigm. The physical sciences have as a result come to seem more insular, except insofar as economics – or at least one substantial branch of it – is becoming virtually indistinguishable from applied mathematics.

Within the sciences themselves, the possibility may be opening up of a very different process of unification, brought about less by changes in what Geertz called 'the way we think about the way we think' than by the exigencies of inadequate research funding. When money was relatively plentiful, it was seen as important in most scientific fields to be actively involved in empirical work. Those who concentrated instead on the synoptic and theoretical aspects of research tended to be viewed as parasitic on the workers at the coal face, doing (as one of my interviewees said) 'damned little work for their syntheses', or taking (in the words of another) 'a cheap and easy way out'. The emphasis was on exploration rather than consolidation: on opening up more and more new seams to be mined, as against asking where the process was leading and what its relative significance might be. Progressive fragmentation into one new specialism after another was, one might say, promoted at the expense of any concern with coherence and reflection. Perhaps, however, the increasing constraints on laboratory-based and field-based research may persuade some scientists to review and synthesise existing findings as an alternative to keeping up with the latest fashionable topic. In this way, more coherent sense might be made of what is already known.

Leaving aside changes in intellectual perspective or in the political and financial context of research, there are at least two other significant developments which demand attention in the UK context. The first is the slow, but now seemingly inexorable, broadening of the secondary school curriculum; the second, a change (related both to this and to the shortage of research funding) in the relative status of teaching as against research. As far as the first is concerned, all the expectations are that the reduction which is called for by the 1988 Education Act in the presently excessive degree of specialisation from the age of 14 onwards will result in a comparable change in undergraduate provision. There is already a significant range of modular degree programmes, joint honours courses and multidisciplinary offerings of various kinds. One would expect the move from the standard closely-defined single-subject honours pattern to gather momentum as more and more university entrants are drawn either from less specialised upper school programmes, more broadly-based vocational courses, or general entry on the basis of relevant work experience. On the whole, it might be predicted that the less elitist recruitment to higher education becomes, the less viable the tendency will prove to regard undergraduate programmes as first and foremost a preparation for a research career in a particular discipline. Such a change may do something through the broadening of curricula to promote a less narrowly specialised intellectual framework among existing teachers in higher education, as well as helping to ensure that future generations of academics will have a wider cognitive background than those brought up within the confines of a single subject field.

By general admission, the reward system in universities has been heavily skewed in favour of research – or perhaps one should say the ability to get work published – and against teaching. Various changes have begun, even if only modestly, to adjust this imbalance. One is the greater premium placed on pedagogic competence in a context in which students can no longer be assumed to be both highly qualified and drawn from the top ten percentile of ability. Another is the effect of the already-mentioned limitation on research funding.

Fewer and fewer academics can now expect – as they have traditionally done in UK universities – to have at least a quarter of their total
time available for research, together with a further allocation for
study leave of up to one term in seven. Those no longer so privileged
understandably demand better recognition for their teaching activities. A third factor is the growing political pressure for accountability
in higher education and in particular for what is fashionably labelled
as 'quality assurance' in relation to teaching. One of the most notice-
able features of undergraduate teaching – which is often the subject
of positive comment even among those who are most active in
research – is that it necessarily demands a widening of one's mental
perspective, drawing one out of the confines of one's current intellectual obsession and enforcing some contact – which is at times
found to be highly beneficial – with other ideas. It is not perhaps
unduly optimistic to expect that a combination of broader undergraduate curricula with an enhanced emphasis on teaching might
have the effect of reducing, even if not of eliminating, the parochial-
ism of current research practice.

Barriers to progress

At this point, having suggested that the omens are more favourable
for the development of a coherent intellectual community than they
have been over the last generation at least, I want to draw attention
to two interrelated sets of attitudes which are prevalent in the scholarly world and which serve to perpetuate and reinforce the insularity
of, and hostility between, different subject-based communities. The
first of these is the academic equivalent of the jingoism and xenopho-
bia which besets particular nations at various times. Just as the 'little
Englander' – more, alas, a reality than a mere legend – could be
characterised by the slogan 'my country, right or wrong', so too there
are more than an eccentric minority of academic staff who live out
the counterpart motto, 'my discipline, right or wrong'. And just as
the most bigoted anti-semite will proudly assert that 'some of my best
friends are Jews', so too academics who have personal acquaintances
in other subject fields will nonetheless continue to pillory those
associated with such fields and to denigrate their competence, if not
their intellectual integrity.

When I was trying to understand, in the course of my recent
research, what were the distinguishing cultural features of different
academic fields, I spent some time in the early stages asking people
in each disciplinary area to give me their own impressions of what
colleagues in other particular subject areas were like (Becher 1981).

What struck me in carrying out this exercise was not only how ignorant each group was of what the others did and how they did it, but also how negative and dismissive their stereotypes were. To give just a few examples, biologists were said by one respondent to be 'ethereal folk who spend time cutting up flowers and being very delicate'; one interviewee was under the impression that the main function of sociologists was to teach social workers; physicists were said variously to be clever but incomprehensible, introverted, paranoic and defensive, technocratic and conservative; and engineers to be dull, conformist, mercenary, unacademic, uncultured and 'technocrats with no refinement'. It must be emphasised that these comments were made, not by hostile outsiders but by people who worked in the same institutions as many of those they wrote off in this way. The incomprehension of, and antagonism towards, those with different perspectives and values seem depressingly reminiscent of members of rival fundamentalist religious sects. Nor is this finding confined to my own research. In reporting an entirely independent study, based on the University of Melbourne, Kay Harman (1990) writes 'misconceptions, stereotyping of outsiders, misunderstandings and contested views were common within and between the cultural coteries of the disciplines and their sub-specialty areas, so making shared activity and dialogue between different groups difficult, if not impossible, at times.'

Such attitudes are I believe closely linked with another phenomenon: the ladder of power and status in academia. There is a long-standing tendency to accord high regard to knowledge domains which are hard, abstract and amenable to mathematical modelling, and to play down those which are soft, qualitative and applied. The degree of academic class-consciousness is heightened in a society like the UK's which is itself heavily class-ridden, but it can also be discerned in other academic systems. There seems to be a crude set of equations underpinning the ladder of esteem, ranging from mathematics and physics at the top, through chemistry and biology to economics and thence to historical and literary studies, finally descending through sociology and engineering to the lower rungs of subject areas such as education, nursing and social work. Purity, it seems, in conjunction with a high level of theorising, represents the pinnacle of intellectual activity. Because abstraction is difficult, it is associated with the achievement of high standards, and offers a benchmark for academic excellence, to which other forms of enquiry approximate in varying degrees.

Unlike some of the issues earlier identified as standing in the way of a closer-knit academic community, these two – the prevalence of partisanship and the influence of disciplinary pecking orders – are amenable to correction by educative measures. That is to say, they may be counteracted by encouraging scholars to recognise the immaturity of, and lack of intellectual basis for, the attitudes behind them. In the case of the caste system, that battle may already be halfway won. One by-product of the Thatcher years in Britain was to introduce a rival calculus of merit based on utility, under which money, student numbers and the status associated with both began to flow in the direction of subjects, such as business studies and engineering, which had previously earned a poor rating. To a certain extent, the earlier status pattern was reversed. In the subsequent process of readjustment from the excesses of the enterprise culture, the chance at least exists to demonstrate that such hierarchies of esteem are not soundly based on intrinsic merit, but rather operate as a crude means of allocating privilege without bothering to adjudicate worth. There is no reason why one subject field should lay claim to automatic preferential treatment over another, as the recent debates about scientific research funding have begun to show (the large amounts of money going into high energy physics, at the expense of other less prestigious scientific specialisms, are increasingly resented).

Finding the common ground

To eliminate the grounds for academic snobbery is itself to weaken the basis for disciplinary insularity. In a relatively classless society, the tendency to envy or despise those of higher or lower status, and in any case to dislike and distrust those outside one's own clique, is conveniently reduced. There are already some academic groupings which have managed to generate, in socio-political terms, a sense of collective unity. The physicists – despite the high degree of cognitive fragmentation mentioned earlier – are an example in the natural sciences, as are the historians in the humanities. What has now to be sought for is an extension of this principle of internal coherence into the wider domain of the disciplines at large. That may sound like a tall order, but it is I would suggest something that could be achieved by a systematic, well-orchestrated and step-by-step campaign.

One possible strategy is to find ways of promoting and publicising what might be called disciplinary multilingualism. People who can operate effectively in the context of two or more different intellectual settings have more than two strings to their bow, since they may also find opportunities to work in the borderlands between the two. There are likely to be more such people as specialisation diminishes up to bachelor's degree level. Another strategy is to encourage inter- and intra-disciplinary mobility. This already exists to a quite surprising degree: my interviews in various subject fields brought to light several interesting instances, including a chemist who had migrated to biology, an anthropologist in a history department, a plant pathologist who had made a new career in studying fish vision and a literature specialist who had switched from sixteenth-century poetry to modern drama. What may be particularly useful here is the intellectual counterpart of easier travel between countries: something perhaps along the lines of short-term secondment opportunities at least to visit, and perhaps even on occasion to work in, departments in other subject areas than one's own. The resulting academic interchange could be reinforced and underpinned by the equivalent of travel literature, describing aspects of life in particular intellectual domains as seen by an outside observer.

Whether or not there is considered to be a strong enough case for a conscious campaign along some such lines as these, Kay Harman's study, to which reference was made earlier, reminds us that:

> more enlightened understanding of the bases of cultural differences between disciplines could lead to more effective dialogue and greater respect between individuals and groups for the different ways people approach problems and the different intellectual styles they adopt... plans to reconstruct higher education that are based on cross-cultural collaboration or interdisciplinary linkages will have little chance of success if the bases of the differences are not well understood. (Harman 1990)

This discussion has dwelt, to a large extent, on the difficulties in the way of creating a more harmonious and coherent scholarly community, and the divisions which serve to fragment the inhabitants of academe. But it would seem appropriate to conclude with the observation that things may in any case not be as bad as they can appear in our more gloomy moments. To quote Kay Harman once again:

> While on the surface academics appeared divided and fragmented, underneath lay a stubborn core of unity. Detected from an emerging babel of conflicting voices, divergent interests and divided loyalties, were aspects of a common culture which encapsulated a deeply entrenched, 'unwritten' occupational ethos. (Harman 1990)

She goes on to spell out some of the familiar features of that occupational ethos, echoing Burton Clark's earlier analysis of the academic profession (Clark 1987a, b).

Those who wish for a detailed account of her findings should refer to the original text. Here are a few samples, merely to give a flavour of the shared principles she enumerates:

Knowledge should know no bounds – all aspects of the recognised branches of learning should be open to enquiry and the ideas of younger members should be just as valued as those of their elders.

The branches of learning should be formally equal, or at least legitimate forms of knowledge, i.e. they should speak with the same authority because of their specialised knowledge base.

There should be a free exchange of ideas in a context where uncertainty and contradiction are tolerated.

Intellectual conflict should remain separate from personal or social conflict.

As in all implicit or explicit codes of conduct, salient principles are more honoured in the breach than in the observance. But for all the evident differences, it is clear that there are also many important similarities between those who occupy and defend their different scholarly arenas. There is indeed a subterranean sense of commonality which is there to be unearthed. The cause of unity is far from being a lost one.

References

Becher, T. (1981) Towards a definition of disciplinary cultures. *Studies in Higher Education 6*, 2, 109–122.

Becher, T. (1989) *Academic Tribes and Territories*. Milton Keynes: Open University.

Becher, T. (1990) The counter-culture of specialisation. *European Journal of Education 25*, 3, 333–346.

Boden, M. (1991) The contours of the mind. *University of Sussex Annual Report 1989–90*. University of Sussex.

Buchanan, J.M. (1966) Economics and its scientific neighbours. In S.R. Krupp (ed) *The Structure of Economic Science*. Englewood Cliffs, NJ.: Prentice Hall.

Bucher, R. and Strauss, A. (1961) Professions in process. *American Journal of Sociology 66*, 325–334.

Campbell, D.T. (1969) Ethnocentrism of disciplines and the fish-scale model of omniscience. In M. Sherif and C. Sherif (eds) *Interdisciplinary Relationships in the Social Sciences*. Aldine.

Clark, B.R. (1987a) *The Academic Life*. Princeton: Princeton University Press.

Clark, B.R. (ed) (1987b) *The Academic Profession*. Berkeley: University of California Press.

Geertz, C. (1980) Blurred genres. *The American Scholar 49*, 165–178.

Harman, K. (1990) Culture and conflict in academic organisation. *Journal of Educational Administration 27*, 3, 30–54.

Klein, J.T. (1990) *Interdisciplinarity*. Wayne State University Press.

Lindblom, C.E. (1959) The science of muddling through. *Public Administration Review 19*, 155–169.

Mulkay, M. (1974) Conceptual displacements and migration in science. *Science Studies 4*, 205–234.

Mulkay, M. (1977) The sociology of the scientific research community. In J. Spiegel-Rösing and D. de S. Price (eds) *Science, Technology and Society*. London: Sage.

Needham, J. (1956–1988) *Science and Civilization in China*, Vols 1–6. Cambridge: Cambridge University Press.

Pinch, T. (1990) The culture of scientists and disciplinary rhetoric. *European Journal of Education, 25*, 3, 295–304.

Popper, K. (1966) *The Open Society and its Enemies Fifth Edition*. London: Routledge.

Ruscio, K.P. (1985) *Specializations in academic disciplines. Mimeo: University of California, Los Angeles, Comparative Higher Education Research Group*.

Wittgenstein, L. (1953) *Philosophical Investigations*. Oxford: Blackwell.

Chapter 5

Towards a Common/Universal Language

Kenneth Wilson

Introduction: aims and values

Two recently published volumes prompt a general reflection on our age: Noel Annan's *Our Age* (1990) and Kenneth Morgan's *The People's Peace* (1990). The former suggests, at the very least, that a serious lack of moral integrity (even sensitivity) lay at the heart of the education of those from the Universities of Oxford and Cambridge and the London School of Economics who came to influence or determine policy in the years 1929–79. In *The People's Peace*, Professor Morgan traces between 1945 and 1989 the vicissitudes of the political, economic and social meanderings of a society which lacked unity or purpose. In both cases, the report of a management consultant might include reference to the need for a mission statement and the importance of getting everyone on to a single agenda. In both cases, it could be argued, we have adequate grounds for understanding the rise and prominence of Thatcherism with its attendant principles, compromises and fudges. At least there was a genuine attempt to lead, to direct and to delegate. But there was hardly a common language even there, as is clear from an examination of, say, either economic or education policy over this period.

Many discussions in the Seventies of the 'politics of envy' assumed that socialism was not so much intent upon improving the quality of life for the least advantaged as it was concerned to restrict the enjoyment of the majority; perhaps in this socialism was showing itself to be the true heir of Calvinism, non-conformity and the non-conformist conscience. More recently, we have experienced the 'politics of greed', as if the mere possession and control of wealth, with the power and privilege that attends such a position, is all that matters. In both cases it has been hard to see that attention to ideals, to moral concern, to personal integrity or to the common good has been the prime concern. There has been little vision, little perspective and little coherence in our recent experience; above all, there has been no common language of discussion, discrimination or concern, nor therefore, above all, any shared values as a basis for a common life.

How, therefore, are we to build a satisfactory education system to meet the demands of such conflicting values? No wonder there is a conflict between a child-centred school experience and a subject-based curriculum: an apparent conflict which I find as perplexing to understand as it is to address. On the one hand, there can surely be no education which is not concerned with the nature of the being, the human, who is to be educated, and the individual circumstances of the person who is wanting to teach or to learn. On the other hand, without a precise and interested knowledge of the nature and content of the disciplines of enquiry into which a pupil is to be introduced and with which, in association with the teacher, he or she is to be engaged in conversation, there can be no such thing as education either. But this apparent conflict is not solved by the introduction of a National Curriculum in schools, and the development of testing or assessment, apart from attention also to the aims and purposes of education and the values which underlie it. It is interesting that there is even now discussion of a core curriculum in higher education, presumably with the same lack of concern for the overall purposes of education.

Now it may be that we needed a national curriculum (I believe we did) and even that we should benefit from having a core curriculum in higher education. Certainly, there could be much to gain from discussing what the content of such a core would be. What is, however, hard to see, is the usefulness of such a discussion or development unless we recognize that it implies the importance of discussing the aims and purposes of education. We should not be put off by those, and there are some, who say that whenever anyone wants to promote the discussion of the aims and purposes of education they reach for their guns. Such frustration of the integrity of intellectual enquiry is no more to be accepted than the invasion of a small country by a militant, indifferent, ambitious and aggressive neighbour.

Discussion of education in any society is necessarily related to the understanding which that society has, or believes itself to have, of its history, nature and purpose. To discuss education is therefore to bring society into touch with its values; in order to be in a position to do this sensibly, it must attend to the possibility of creating a common/universal language.

Education and coherence

There is a journal called *Viz* which is readily available in station newsstands. It is, it seems, the most sexually explicit, morally indifferent and blasphemous publication on general release at the moment. It is ostentatiously humiliating to women and proposes an entirely instrumentalist and destructive view of anything which might require thought or reflection. It appears that it is enormously popular and sells most of its copies to those who might on other grounds be regarded as educated. By 'educated' here I mean those who possess or are reading for degrees in higher education. Ought we to be worried? Does an expression of concern imply an identification with the right or with an old-fashioned perspective which suggests that standards (whatever they are) are falling? Higher education is not concerned with mere competences, but with the quality of person who is produced by the process and his or her capacity to contribute to the essential, moral purposes of society. As teachers, whatever we teach, we are involved with this fundamental purpose of all human enquiry. How can we reasonably hold ourselves professionally responsible for anything other than our own ability to stimulate interest in a discipline for its own sake?

It may be difficult, but we can and should: indeed, as a matter of fact we are held accountable by society precisely in this broad way. Thus teachers in school are blamed not merely because standards in computational skill are less than the average employer would like, but because there is hooliganism at football matches, litter in the streets, and rudeness on public transport. We also are held accountable for the failures in understanding which make doctors less helpful to their patients, teachers less interested in their pupils, and too many of our students inarticulate and unable to get on with others. Now we may or may not be actually to blame, and even if we are to blame, circumstances may or may not tend to make the situation excusable; but the point is that employers, parents, friends, politicians, editors and writers of letters to the press do tend to hold us responsible. Indeed, we are seen ourselves to be more of an interest group who contribute to the babble of languages rather than a concerned focus of discussion which might heal division and bring about a new understanding of what might constitute the common good. Educators are not obviously regarded as a community of scholars concerned to attend to things for their own sake and to recommend to others those things which are life-enhancing and in the interests of society at large.

What is clear is that even amongst ourselves we do not have a perspective which can be identified as bringing coherence to our purposes as scholars, researchers, teachers and administrators in Higher Education. There are three divisions in particular to which I wish to draw attention. First, there is the division between research and teaching. No one can teach who is not enquiring; though, of course, such enquiring may not of itself be sufficient as to make a major contribution to the sum total of human knowledge. But by 'new knowledge' we frequently appear to mean no more than originality – and originality is an overrated commodity. Mere originality never achieved anything except notoriety in any field of human endeavour, whether that be scholarship or the entertainment industry. On the other hand, genuine research which adds opportunity to human life by increasing our understanding of ourselves, our ability to relate to one another and our world, is worth its weight in gold. But then so is that teaching which enables us to remember for good the contributions of the past, which reminds us of opportunities yet unaccepted and which celebrates the knowledge, virtue and intelligence which is already a part of our human experience. Indeed, apart from such good teaching, we will take for granted many things which will, like love in a marriage, simply disappear if we do not work at them. And in order to work at them, we need to have the language in which to talk about them. The ways in which the Etruscan language shaped and formed the human experience of Etruscans is lost to us because we have neither the language nor the literature of these peoples. That may or may not matter: how can we know? We do know that it matters when we lose the capacity to recognise and develop the knowledge, virtues and values which have shaped, if not consciously then unconsciously, our lives and do so still.

Thus our failure to recognise the nature of mediaeval civilisation was in part caused by the cataclysmic divisions which materialised in the sixteenth century and which meant that for the protestant it had to be the case that in the past the individual was crushed by a monolithic church and that all that was good for the human came with the rebirth of the human individual from that century onwards. Researches into mediaeval philosophy and theology[1] combined with the emergence of new areas of enquiry including the way people represented themselves through gesture for example, all combine to show that the language of the mediaeval period was misunderstood

---

1   Of course the Latin of many of the texts complicated matters, as the vernacular triumphed in Church and State. But for a brilliant attempt to unpack the language and to 'say' what St Thomas Aquinas said in ways which are both linguistically coherent with the original and philosophically illuminating without being technical, see the concise translation of *Summa Theologiae* (McDermott 1989).

and distorted and the realities which it expressed eventually lost until very recent times.[2]

A teaching purpose which maintains and develops the best of what we already know is as crucial for our well-being as a research focus; the two are complementary, not in conflict.

Purposes and levels

Second, there is the apparent conflict between the professional, vocational or practical purpose, and the intention to study a subject for its own sake. There has been a particular structural dimension to this in our own recent experience given the binary line favoured by Anthony Crosland and the two former funding Councils, the Universities Funding Council and the Polytechnics and Colleges Funding Council. This bifurcation is not unrelated to the former point, but is different in feel and in implication. Thus, the polytechnics and colleges are teaching institutions, whose purposes are practical, professional and vocational. They are to be contrasted with the universities, which are funded for research and only because of their eminence in this context are they qualified also to be teaching institutions. Such divisions were hard to maintain and have come to an end rather sooner than many had envisaged. However, there is a major point.

Given that it would be possible to provide a mission statement for each institution of higher education, whether university, polytechnic or college, could we assume that there could be properly constructed statements which had on the one hand no reference to practice, and on the other no reference to the value of enquiry for its own sake? I submit that it would be impossible. One could indeed have a research institute which was concerned with nothing but enquiry for its own sake; one could have a technical institute which did nothing but drill its members in professional practice. But neither would be regarded as an institution of higher education. Indeed, even in their own terms, one expects that researchers in a research institute will question the

---

2   cf. Le Goff (1964 p.viii): It seems to me that the development of ideas about the Middle Ages and the deepening of researches and reflections have reinforced two of the fundamental standpoints of this book. On the one hand, the middle ages, a period of violence, of harsh living conditions, dominated by the natural world, was also a period of exceptional creativity and laid the foundations of the development of western civilisation. On the other hand, even more than others, perhaps, the society of the mediaeval west can only be understood if one shows how its material, social and political realities were penetrated by symbolism and the imaginary world. Only the study of how people represented themselves alongside the study of the way in which they thought and felt can allow us to understand this world which we lost not so very long ago, *and which still permeates our minds and imaginations.*

moral dimensions of its enquiry processes and the moral nature of the enquiry *per se*. And at the same time, the technologists working in a technical institute will be expected to form an opinion about the truth and falsity of the basic assumptions behind the techniques which it is inculcating in its members.

But there is more to it than this. A university cannot avoid responsibility for the choice of topics into which it encourages research, for the styles of teaching which it promotes, for the quality of the relationships which characterise the administrative and pedagogical communities, and the ultimate value to the community at large of those who graduate. And while this has had a special focus recently because of the emphasis on the cash transactions involved, it is implicit in the very nature of the institutions themselves. We in higher education are equipping students so that they can find employment which is valuable to society and themselves in the long as well as the short term.

To put the matter directly, any discipline which is worth studying for its own sake, is worth studying because it is at any rate in the long term in the interests of society to have students studying it. And any profession which has a body of knowledge and professional skills associated with its practice should be involved in higher education in order to be subject to the critical environment found there: it is in the interests of society that professions be so integrated. Higher education has a responsibility in both contexts and an interest in maintaining and developing their fundamental not accidental association.

A third apparent dichotomy assumes a dissociation of levels and of contexts. Thus there is primary education and higher education, formal and informal education, and the role of business and government in education. Until we see these as continuous, overlapping and mutually supportive we shall find it hard if not impossible to create or rediscover a common language. The fact that I can receive references still for prospective primary school teachers which suggest that while X is not very good academically and lacks confidence in public and with his or her peer group, the applicant is nevertheless splendid with young children and will make an ideal primary school teacher, just about sums it up. In my judgement, the intellectual demands on the primary school teacher are commensurate at least with those demanded of any teacher in higher education and if the teacher is not capable of learning in a critical and ordered way from the experience of teaching (i.e. capable of engaging in what might reasonably be called research) he or she ought not to be regarded as a professional. Of course there is, as David Hargreaves and others have indicated, plenty of room for ancillary roles in education as in medicine or the law; I am talking here of the genuinely professional teacher.

Primary education is not a preliminary to secondary education, or that to higher education; each offers experience, knowledge and skills which underpin and are structurally vital to what comes after. It is in all our interests, for example, to get the first two right if we genuinely value the latter, not because they precede and are left behind in higher education, but because they are inherently a part of it.

It is about time we ceased to regard industry as the means whereby we merely earn the money to support education: it is intimately concerned with education, its values, its content, its processes and its length. We are not competitors for scarce resources for our own private but useful purposes, we are collaborators in developing opportunities for the future, the judgement to inform good choices, the critical discipline to identify and reject bad choices, and above all to identify and celebrate the values which will make for a humane and confident human society in the future.

The need for a coherent stance to underlie our approach to all these matters is apparent. Such an approach requires that we pursue the possibility of rediscovering or creating a universal language in which to talk of them.

Mirages of order

There have been many attempts to pursue just such a mirage. A brief discussion of some of them will indicate just how difficult and how complex the task could be and, what is more, how naive the quest might seem in itself to be.

One strategy is to identify some bogey in the immediate past, perhaps some foreign interloper, and then to set about rediscovering and reimposing some earlier structure which one fondly imagines to have existed in some perfect form. Thus, for example, there was amongst some of those involved in the civil war of the seventeenth century an assumption that all their troubles stemmed from the alien feudal law introduced by William the Conqueror and his Norman followers, and which superseded the Ancient Constitution of the Anglo-Saxon period in which all their rights as subjects had been guaranteed. In order to bring about the brave new world, therefore, all that was needed was the reintroduction of those legal rights found in the Ancient Constitution and the rejection of the feudal law. Now, we know that not only was there no such Ancient Constitution, but that what law and constitution was in existence in Anglo-Saxon times did not give citizens or barons the rights which many wished to claim for themselves as citizens in the seventeenth century. There was no common language or tradition of that kind on which to draw (cf. Pocock 1957).

Another strategy is to reject the past as essentially misleading and thus to believe that it offers no illuminating criteria by which to evaluate present experience or therefore to provide any delineation of future possibilities. What in this case we need to recognise is that individuals can take the future into their own hands and find their own personal (and perhaps private) salvation. Hence Protestantism can supersede Catholicism as then understood and interpreted in part, and the individual believer can enter heaven without the intervention of priests or benefit of Church or sacraments. But what crucial loss of common language or even any sense that one was needed was involved in this huge change! Hence the problems of Descartes, the privatisation of experience, the problem of certainty and the mirage of a public world.

Now individuals, of course, have miniscule influence when seen as mere specks in the emerging capitalist spectrum or within the royal prerogative, especially when that was conceived to be divinely ordained. Hence the attraction of a class perspective to make a new world and a new future for itself; never mind the interests of other persons. And so the French Revolution, with the ultimate emergence of Marxism, looks to a future wholly created anew and not dependent on the past, except in the sense that there is a metaphysic of the historical process which properly understood can be cooperated with so as to make the triumph of the working class inevitable.

Such a prospect was all the more attractive given the rise of science and technology and the power which they offered to human beings to control the material world and to make the future look like the desired end. A new world was indeed in the hands of the new society, and the new society in the hands of the new class.

The desirability of a common language for either of these perspectives is obvious: the personal/individual and the class; each had one by definition in the contrasting but hardly contradictory languages of Christianity and Marxism. There are many issues here, but these traditions of reflection suffered from the fact that it was in the interests of persons to deny their inherent community of concern individually and to institutionalise their differences in Catholic and Protestant structures on the one hand, and orthodoxy and revisionism on the other. Sometime it will occur to someone to compare and contrast the role and work of John XXIII and Gorbachev, for each in his own way sought to bring the musty formed opinions which result from past discussion and confusion into conversation with a world

of new priorities and interests. As Gorbachev himself said in a speech
to the Nineteenth All-Union Conference of the Communist party on
28th June, 1988, 'In short, comrades, what we are talking about is a
new role for public opinion in the country. And there is no need to
fear the novel, unconventional character of some opinions...'

But there are other ways of finding a universal language and
bringing it to bear on our human affairs; most of them are reductionist
in one way or another. The ambiguity of language may itself be
regarded as inherent with the consequence that only ostensive definition is acceptable. The search for transparent truth through the
picture theory of atomic propositions as the ultimate basis of all
knowledge was too ambitious even for Wittgenstein to bring to
fruition. Perhaps we have to live with the indefinability of the empirical basis of our knowledge, perhaps it is indeed part of our
responsibility as humans so to do.

If there is not a secure unambiguous empirical basis for our
language, then maybe there is a secure common logic for our mildly
ambiguous languages. The interest in basic logics, in axiomatisation,
in identifying the logical basis of mathematical enquiry (itself, of
course, a common language of modelling for our empirical enquiries)
has been significant since Boole and Frege; and yet the identification
or creation of a fundamental logic of this kind in which all and every
structural relationship of style and argument can be expressed seems
not only illusory but possibly inconsistent with our experience.

There have, too, been attempts to develop artificial natural languages as means to cultivate international and community understanding. Esperanto is the one which has been most promoted, but
notwithstanding its limited success, hardly anyone regards it as
having the capacity even to develop in such a way as to enable
individuals or societies to express creatively their full sense of what
it is to be human in relation to one another, the world and themselves.
A lemma of this argument is that form of reductionism which sees
science, economics, history or sociology as the key to the understanding of all things, and the respective language of each discipline
as the language into which all others can be translated or at least with
regard to which all other languages can be expressed. I suspect that
this view is less widely held than it has been, though there is much
in the policy decisions of many to suggest that it lies behind much
thinking. Even if the view is more than the simple formula that
science encompasses all reality, it still assumes that science offers us
insight into the 'real' nature of the world; and the same could be said
of economics or sociology.

The desire for a common language is powerfully apparent even
in conflict, where a reason for it is often profoundly based in the need

which one group feels because of insecurity or inadequacy to dominate another. The most obvious process here is to require others to
speak your language, so as to enforce the values implicit in it. The
essential attractiveness of a universal language is clear.

A possible framework

The very terms university and college are significant. They suggest
the importance of bringing things together and of keeping them
whole. What I propose in the rest of this chapter bears directly upon
this matter and upon the specific dimension of the religious tradition
which gave birth to our thirst for knowledge and consequent understanding of our particular role in the world. I make no apology for
the fact that this is overtly theological and, indeed, Christian, in scope
and intent. I hope that the reasons for this emerge as empirical and
logical and not as matters of prejudice, let alone exclusive claims for
truth. Theological discourse is chosen as illustrative, not definitive.

It was the demands of church and state which in this country gave
rise to what we would now call the institutions of higher education,
namely the Universities of Oxford and Cambridge. These religious
foundations assumed a theological basis for all teaching and learning,
whether in arts, law, medicine or in the faculty of theology itself. It
was this language, or set of languages, which provided the commonality of discourse. Indeed, the intellectual tasks were not so much the
holding together of differing and contrasting disciplines of enquiry
as the development of the common language in the light of these
enquiries so as to show how the common discussion could grow and
continue. This discussion produced suitably qualified persons to
serve both king and bishop. The clerks were in communication with
each other and in principle with all the various disciplines of intellectual enquiry and professional practice.

However, the failure of the language of theology to grow to
encompass new areas of enquiry, and the assumption on the part of
many that it was in principle incapable of doing so in such a way as
to offer anything which could reasonably be called explanation, alike
brought about a substantial reduction in confidence in the value of
theological discourse. Thus, not unnaturally, the theological community tended to confine itself to ecclesiastical structures which organised themselves to define their languages for their own institutional
purposes. In particular, predictability and experiment became the
essential virtues of any language which purported to offer true
knowledge of the world and this was consistent with science, but not
with theology, it was believed.

The impact of this thinking was most profoundly felt in the universities where, as Maurice Cowling has pointed out, a post-Christian culture has replaced a Christian one over the course of the last one hundred and fifty or so years (Cowling, 1980, 1985, in press). One does not have to share all Cowling's views in order to see the validity of this point: 'It is from religion that modern English intellectual history should begin. That it does not so begin – that it begins rather with the history of political, philosophical, literary, critical, aesthetic, economic or educational activity, or with religion considered as the history of theology or ecclesiastical history – registers historians' reluctance to give critical consideration to the culture to which they belong. In particular, it registers reluctance to consider the complicated connection between its professional academic character on the one hand and its secular, liberal character on the other (Cowling 1980 p.xii).

Such an attack on the integrity of historians, or at least their inability to tell the wood from the trees, has not gone unanswered. But on what basis can we account for the thirst for knowledge and the institutional structures which embodied it and encouraged it, if not the Christian theological tradition which was, in England at least, its *fons et origo*? We may not want to go as far as John Henry Newman, who said that 'If the Catholic faith is true, a University cannot exist externally to the Catholic pale, for it cannot teach Universal Knowledge if it does not teach Catholic theology', and also that '... a direct and active jurisdiction of the Church over it and in it is necessary, lest it should become the rival of the Church with the community at large in those theological matters which to the Church are exclusively committed – acting as the representative of the intellect, as the Church is the representative of the religious principle' (Newman 1976, p.184). This inherent division between the role of Church and University may not accord with our present prejudices, but it is independent of the fact that a refusal to attend to the desire for coherence which lay behind the beginnings of higher education is a misleading basis on which to reject the vital importance of re-establishing or newly meeting such a coherence now.

We are misled if we think of course that we are ever going to come to the end of the quest, but the quest is not a tangential but an essential ingredient of the work of higher education. In principle, the world is intelligible and all knowledge is one, and it is helpful to have a universal language which allows us to recognise that fact and the fact that it requires a great deal of effort, of observation, of imagination and of intellect to work at the possibility that it might be seen to be so. It is this which a theological language in principle provides.

But that requires a reconsideration of the context, history, practice, status, form and nature of theological enquiry, its methods and doctrines. I offer brief comments on this in what follows.

Thus, through a notion of revelation, there is preserved not the fact that there is knowledge which is only open to the human being as a result of direct communication from God, but that no account of human experience, however complete it may appear, is free of the possibility of development, criticism and even refutation and rejection in the light of new experience or creative reorganistion of existing experience.

A doctrine of creation preserves the view that there is purposeful coherence to the universe of which the human is a part and possibly a focus, and that it is not the accidental holding together of individually separate worlds which could otherwise be accounted for in their own independent terms.

A doctrine of the freedom, unity and uncreated being of God, who is all-powerful and all-loving means that we are not in the business of looking for extraneous other powers or beings in terms of whose activity it is necessary to explain matters which do not apparently fit in with our present prejudices. It was the case that incomplete explanations in the evolutionary process were held to offer God the way into our world; this was a wholly misleading and unhelpful approach. There are those who now wish to account for those experiences which are hurtful or apparently evil as the result of some other God or gods, as if God was either unwilling or unable to accept the blame for it all, or as if we had not the courage to attribute responsibility where it actually lay. This is equally misleading. Like it or not, there is only one God and we had better get on with the job of working out what sort of a God it is who can justly and reasonably want to have created and be responsible for a world of the kind we actually experience.

The doctrine of sin points to the fact that it is often all a bit much for us, and that we prefer as humans to seek power (i.e. to impose our own language on others), to opt out (i.e. to say we can manage by ourselves), or to claim it doesn't matter (i.e. to say that there is no meaning or purpose in it all). Now, this is an intriguing doctrine because of all those open to human enquiry it is the one which in fact most human beings find most obviously true and therefore, paradoxically, most difficult to accept, because of its personal questions. It is not half so easy to accept, for example, as the mere fact of the existence of a God, which opinion polls tell us is one of the most widely shared beliefs in our secularised society.

The doctrine of resurrection suggests that in any situation there are the seeds of new life, at least in the sense that imagination and love will find new prospects and new dimensions for their work. Form does not necessarily or inevitably frustrate substance. But it also suggests that the process is not merely natural: there is a profound difference between immortality and resurrection. The latter requires work, indeed it requires pain and suffering. Thus the human cannot hope to recreate his or her world personally, let alone in community with others, without demanding and testing thought and work which by its very nature may seem threatening.

The doctrine of eschatology suggests that if God is the origin, so he is the end of all that he is involved with in creation. There is no hole at the end of the universe down which everything goes, and no pressure on God which means that he might give up, or find things too much for him. What he has set about in creating, he will continue to the end, because he will never act in a way which is foreign to his nature.

And all this is demonstrated to be consistent with the nature of the world as it is. We can, as humans, learn about ourselves, our world, and learn how in practice to work out the implications of that understanding, so as to fulfil our natures and be true to ourselves and our Creator.

Necessary wholeness

Now, a higher education which encapsulates a language which assumes and celebrates these claims, opennesses and questions, is a possibility. I am not sure that we have one. Of course, I do not imply that the metaphysics of theological language is true, or most particularly that it cannot be discussed or argued about – precisely the opposite. I do claim that it offers encouragement to learn about the world and to put our understanding into the closest possible coherence while not denying difference. It allows us to see ourselves as having genuine opportunities to change our worlds and to develop our understanding: it leaves us responsible and accountable. Further, it shows that there is little that we can do for ourselves, but much that with others is effectable. And it matters what we teach and what we learn, how we teach and how we learn, and what we are and what we become. A higher education which paid attention to these things would be very desirable.

The world of theological discourse enables questions to be asked about human nature, human society and the meaning and purpose of life. If we are as a human community to take responsibility for our possible futures and build an effective education system for all, then some universal discourse of an analogous kind needs to be created;

the fragmented discourses of individual disciplines provide ingredients and perspectives, but not the whole view. Whether this new language will be theological remains to be seen and is not the purpose of this chapter to argue. What I do claim is that in its time and in its own way it allowed questions to be asked which will not go away and which for our own human well-being we need to learn how to ask again in a delightful but threatening and perplexing world.

References

Annan, N. (1990) *Our Age*. London: Weidenfeld and Nicolson.

Cowling, M. (1980) *Religion and Public Doctrine in England, Vol. I*. Cambridge: Cambridge University Press.

Cowling, M. (1985) *Religion and Public Doctrine in England, Vol. II*. Cambridge: Cambridge University Press.

Cowling, M. (in press) *Religion and Public Doctrine in England, Vol. III*. Cambridge: Cambridge University Press.

Le Goff, J. (1964) *Mediaeval Civilisation 400–1500*. (Trans. J. Barrow 1988. Oxford: Blackwell.)

McDermott, T. (1989) *Summa Theologiae - A Concise Translation*. Norwich: Eyre and Spottiswoode.

Morgan, K.O. (1990) *The People's Peace*. Oxford: Oxford University Press.

Newman, J.H. (1976) *The Idea of a University*. (ed) I.T. Ker. Oxford: Clarendon.

Pocock, J.G.A. (1957) *The Ancient Constitution and the Feudal Law*. Cambridge: Cambridge University Press.

Chapter 6

Towards a New Enlightenment
What the Task of Creating Civilisation Has to Learn from the Success of Modern Science

Nicholas Maxwell

Two great problems of learning

Modern academic inquiry suffers from a serious, wholesale, fundamental defect. Though very successful at improving specialised knowledge and technological know-how, it is an intellectual, social and moral disaster when it comes to helping us realise what is of value in life – in particular, when it comes to helping us create a more civilised, enlightened world.[1]

Vastly oversimplifying things, one can say that humanity is confronted by two great problems of learning, namely:

1. learning how to improve knowledge about the world
2. learning how to become civilised or enlightened.

We have solved the first of these problems, but have so far failed to solve the second problem. We have failed to develop traditions and institutions of learning rationally designed to help us realise what is of value, create civilisation.

We solved the essentials of the first great problem of learning when we discovered how to set about progressively improving our knowledge about the world – that is when we created science in the sixteenth and seventeenth centuries. As a result of the work of Kepler, Galileo, Descartes, Huygens, Newton and others, humanity discovered a *method* for the progressive improvement of knowledge about the universe, the famous empirical method of science.

---

1   For earlier arguments in support of this claim see Maxwell (1976, 1980, 1984a, 1984b, 1985, 1986, 1987, 1988, 1991, 1992).

This solution to the problem of learning how to improve knowledge of the universe has been astonishingly successful. It has led to the vastly increased and improved knowledge and understanding of the universe, and of our place in it, that is embodied in modern scientific knowledge. It has also led to modern technology. Scientific knowledge and technological know-how have made possible our modern world, in so many ways so utterly different from life before science. Without modern scientific knowledge and technological know-how, we can scarcely conceive of modern industry, agriculture, medicine, travel, the media and so on: almost every aspect of life has been transformed by industrial development made possible by technological developments made possible by science.

All this has been of immense benefit to many, in all sorts of ways. But it has not resulted in civilisation, in enlightenment. In a civilised world, let us stipulate, elements of justice, peace, democracy and common humanity would prevail. People would not periodically slaughter each other in their millions; they would not allow millions to starve while others live amidst plenty. In our world, however, millions of people *do* periodically slaughter each other; some hundred million people have died in wars so far in the twentieth century. Those of us fortunate enough to live in the first world have benefited enormously from scientific, technological and industrial progress; the benefits are not so obvious for many living in the third world. Something like a fifth of all people alive today live in conditions of abject poverty, without access to safe water, health care, education. UNICEF estimates that fifteen million children die unnecessarily every year from malnutrition or diseases related to malnutrition. Dictatorships are commonplace in Africa, the Middle East and Asia. And until recently, before Mikhail Gorbachev brought the cold war to an end, it even seemed that humanity was set on a course which could only lead to nuclear annihilation.

Clearly, we do not live in a civilised, enlightened world. We are more like scientifically and technologically sophisticated barbarians than civilised people. As Ghandi said when asked what he thought of Western civilisation: 'I think it would be a good idea.'

It is not just that we have not (yet) created a civilised world; we have not yet discovered how to learn how to do this. Indeed, many people hold that it is not possible to create a genuinely civilised world; human nature simply does not permit such a thing. Steps towards genuine global civilisation can at best only be described as uncertain and faltering. We cannot be sure that we will make steady social progress towards an enlightened world in the way in which we can be sure that we will continue to make scientific and technological progress.

We have failed to create global civilisation; and we have failed to discover how to make social progress towards global civilisation. But in addition to this, we have failed even to develop traditions and institutions of learning rationally designed to help us learn how to create a civilised world. It is not unreasonable to suppose that in order to create world civilisation we must *learn* how to do it. This in turn would seem to require good traditions and institutions of learning specifically designed to help humanity learn how to become civilised and enlightened. It is this that we lack. Our schools and universities are *not* designed to enable humanity to become civilised; for many, they are not even *intended* to have this function.

In effect, then, we have discovered how to solve the first great problem of learning, the problem of how we are to learn about the nature of the universe; but we have failed to solve the second great problem of learning, the problem of learning how to become civilised and enlightened.

It is worth noting just how dangerous this situation is likely to be, on quite general grounds.

The result of solving the first great problem of learning is that we develop modern scientific knowledge and technological know-how. Our power to *act* is as a result enormously increased. But in the absence of a solution to the second great problem of learning, we will not have discovered how to act *wisely*. As long as our power to act is limited, due to limited scientific and technological knowledge, lack of wisdom does not matter too much; we are not in a position to do too much damage. But once our power to act has become vastly increased as a result of modern scientific and technological knowledge, lack of wisdom becomes lethal. Many of our characteristic modern problems have arisen because of this lethal combination of enhanced power to act without enhanced wisdom. Population growth, environmental damage, immensely destructive wars, techniques of dictatorial control, are all the outcome of enhanced power to act without enhanced wisdom. Science without civilisation is almost bound to be a thing of mixed blessings.

Once the first great problem of learning has been solved, in brief, it becomes a matter of the utmost urgency to solve the second great problem of learning. This is the great failure of the academic community in the twentieth century: to create a kind of inquiry rationally designed to help humanity learn how to become civilised, enlightened, wise.

I now give my arguments in support of this claim, and my diagnosis and prescription as to what we need to do to develop a kind of academic inquiry better designed to help us cope with the problems of the modern world.

Enlightenment programmes, old and new

What has gone wrong? My claim is that things went badly wrong during the Enlightenment of the eighteenth century, and have never been put right since then.

A crucial point to appreciate is that, in seeking to solve the second of the two great problems of learning, much is to be learnt from the solution that we have already discovered to the first great problem of learning. In other words, in seeking to make social progress towards an enlightened world we should seek to learn from the way science makes intellectual progress towards greater knowledge and understanding of the natural world. This, I claim, is the methodological key to the salvation of humanity.

We may well hold that just this was the basic idea of the Enlightenment of the eighteenth century: to learn from scientific progress how to make social progress towards a better world.[2] Let us call this general idea the *Enlightenment Programme.*

Unfortunately the *philosophes* of the Enlightenment – Voltaire, Diderot, D'Alembert, Condorcet and the others – made two disastrous mistakes in the particular way in which they developed and sought to implement the Enlightenment Programme. These mistakes have never been put right; we are still suffering from them. They are built into academic inquiry as it is constituted today. It is because of these ancient mistakes that academic inquiry today fails to be properly designed from the standpoint of helping us realise what is of value in life; in other words, from the standpoint of helping us create civilisation.

The Enlightenment Programme can be formulated like this:

The Basic Enlightenment Programme

A. Correctly characterise the progress-achieving methodology of natural science.

B. Work out how to apply an appropriately generalised version of this progress-achieving methodology to social life, so that we may make social progress towards an enlightened world in something like the way in which we already make scientific progress towards greater knowledge.

The *philosophes* of the Enlightenment got both these points disastrously wrong. Their hearts were in the right place, but not their heads. The *philosophes* interpreted points (A) and (B) above as follows:

---

2   Two classic works on the Enlightenment are by Cassirer (1951) and Gay (1973).

The Traditional Enlightenment Programme

A1. The progress-achieving methods of natural science are the inductivist methods employed by Newton, as set out in his *Principia*. Laws and theories are to be arrived at by inductivist generalisation from the phenomena, employing the inductive rules of reason formulated by Newton.

B1. The progress-achieving methods of natural science are then to be applied to the task of improving knowledge of social phenomena, the outcome being the creation of social science on analogy with natural science. The assumption here is that the proper way for rational inquiry to help humanity make social progress towards enlightenment is to provide *knowledge* of social phenomena, even perhaps *knowledge* of the laws of social development.

It was this Traditional Enlightenment Programme, encapsulated in points (A1) and (B1), that led to modern academic inquiry. Gradually, during the nineteenth and twentieth centuries, the social sciences, very much as the *philosophes* had conceived them, were developed and established alongside the natural sciences in academic departments in universities all over the world. The result: a kind of inquiry that is restricted to the pursuit of knowledge and technological know-how. Modern academic inquiry may be construed to be the institutional embodiment of the above traditional Enlightenment Programme.

The Traditional Enlightenment Programme was opposed; it was opposed by Romanticism and by what Isaiah Berlin has called 'The Counter-Enlightenment' (Berlin 1979 ch. 1) on the grounds that the Programme put far too much trust in *science* and *reason*, and far too little trust in *art* and *imagination*. This antirationalist opposition has also influenced aspects of modern academic inquiry; it has influenced literary and cultural studies, philosophy, anthropology, and some other branches of social inquiry, such as sociology. This has helped to break up any sense of an overall common purpose to academic inquiry, encompassing both science and the humanities, both rationalist-inspired and romantic-inspired parts of the academic enterprise.

The Traditional Enlightenment Programme has also been opposed by *rationalists*, the objection being not that too much trust is placed in reason, but that the Programme is itself a betrayal of reason, even while claiming to embody it. (Romanticism thus completely misses the point: what is objectionable about the Traditional Enlightenment Programme is that it manifests too *little* reason, not that it manifests too *much!*) In relatively recent times, both Hayek (Hayek 1979) and

Popper (Popper 1961, 1969) have objected to the Programme along these lines.

As Popper's criticisms are vastly superior to Hayek's, I here consider only Popper's criticisms. Popper has criticised a doctrine alluded to in (B1) above, namely *historicism*, the doctrine that social development obeys *laws*, comparable to the *natural laws* governing the solar system, the task of social science being to discover the laws of social development so that humanity may help the process along. And Popper has criticised the inductivist conception of scientific method referred to in (A1) above. As distinct improvements over (A1) and (B1), Popper has argued for the following:

The Popperian Enlightenment Programme

A2. The progress-achieving method of science is the method of *conjecture and refutation*, the method of putting forward bold guesses which are then subjected to the critical onslaught of attempted empirical falsification, the nub of the empirical method of science. There can be no empirical verification in science, and there is no such thing as induction (Popper 1959, 1963).

B2. The progress-achieving method of natural science is to be applied to the task of improving knowledge of social phenomena, social science being methodologically similar to natural science. Furthermore, social science seeks to acquire knowledge of sociological laws, which are of the same type as physical laws, *neither* being laws of development or evolution (Popper 1961).

Popper's criticisms of the Traditional Programme are decisive; there can be no doubt that Popper's revised Programme is a distinct improvement. But it is not good enough; and Popper's criticisms of the Traditional Programme do not go nearly far enough.

Even though Popper breaks with what were once traditional views of science in rejecting induction and verification, there is a sense in which the whole *raison d'etre* of Popper's positive view is to defend what may be held to be the core of the empiricist creed, namely: 'the *principle of empiricism* which asserts that in science, only observation and experiment may decide upon the *acceptance or rejection* of scientific statements, including laws and theories' (Popper 1963 p.54). But as long as one clings to this highly traditional principle, one cannot solve the problem of induction, the problem, that is, of exhibiting science as rational. In science persistent preference is given to unifying, explanatory theories over disunified, *ad hoc*, non-explanatory theories, to the extent even of violating empirical con-

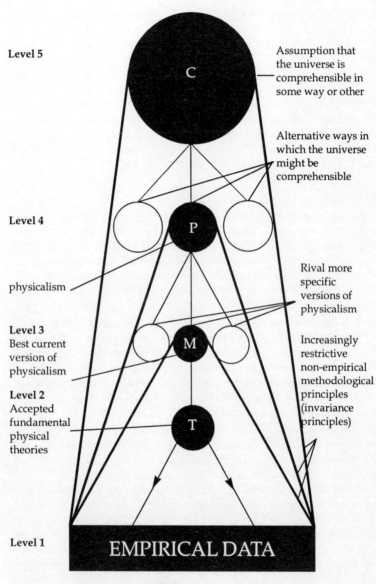

Level 5

C

Assumption that
the universe is
comprehensible in
some way or other

Alternative ways in
which the universe
might be
comprehensible

Level 4

P

physicalism

Rival more
specific
versions of
physicalism

Level 3
Best current
version of
physicalism

M

Increasingly
restrictive
non-empirical
methodological
principles
(invariance
principles)

Level 2
Accepted
fundamental
physical
theories

T

Level 1

EMPIRICAL DATA

Current scientific knowledge
represented by:

Figure 6.1: Aim-orientated empiricism

siderations. This happens to such an extent, indeed, that given any accepted physical theory, such as quantum theory say, there will always be infinitely many rival theories, all easy to formulate, which will fit the available evidence better than the accepted theory: these infinitely many better confirmed theories are rejected so decisively in scientific practice that they are not even formulated, let alone considered. This means that a substantial assumption about the nature of the world is persistently implicit in scientific choice of theories, in scientific method. Intellectual rigour requires that this substantial implicit assumption be made explicit, so that it can be criticised and, we may hope, improved. This leads to a conception of scientific method quite different from Popper's.[3] Its bare bones are depicted in Figure 6.1.

The key point is that science must conjecture that the universe is comprehensible in some way or other, the basic aim of science being the inherently problematic one of discovering in what precise way the universe is comprehensible. In order to pursue this problematic aim rationally, it is essential to explore rival more and less specific versions of the basic aim, each version having its own more or less specific metaphysics and corresponding methods. Rival research programmes need to be pursued within the overall research programme of discovering in what precise way the universe is comprehensible. This leads to evolving aims and methods within a framework of a fixed aim and fixed metamethods. As knowledge improves, knowledge about how to improve knowledge improves as well, this vital feature of scientific rationality helping to explain the explosive growth of scientific knowledge.

Popper's conception of scientific method, encapsulated in (A2), is seriously inadequate in that it misconstrues the basic aim of science to be truth (rather than the more problematic truth-presupposed-to-be-comprehensible) and so fails to do justice to the way more specific aims and methods *evolve* as problems associated with the basic aim are resolved.

Popper's response to the second part of the traditional Enlightenment Programme, namely (B1), is even more inadequate than his response to the first part, namely (A1). Popper is right to point out that laws in physics, such as Newton's law of gravitation, $F = Gm_1m_2/d^2$, are not laws of temporal evolution, even though a combination of such laws together with initial conditions may, in certain circumstances, predict the evolution of an isolated system,

---

3   For the development of this view, see Maxwell (1972, 1974, 1976, 1977, 1979, 1980, 1984a, 1993a, 1994c).

such as the solar system. Popper is right, therefore, to argue that, if social science is to be analogous to physical science, it cannot lead to the discovery of laws of social development, but must rather develop laws like those of physics. Notice however that this very argument assumes that social science ought to be analogous to physical science. It assumes, even more basically, that the proper task of social inquiry is the scientific study of society, on analogy with the scientific study of Nature. Both assumptions are wrong: there are no sociological laws analogous to physical laws;[4] the proper basic task of social inquiry is *not* to improve knowledge of social phenomena (the basic theme of Maxwell 1984a).

The central task of the Enlightenment Programme, remember, is to enable us to learn from scientific progress how to achieve social progress towards enlightenment. The aim is not to make progress in knowledge of social phenomena, progress in social science; it is, rather, to make social progress towards enlightenment, towards world civilisation. We want to get into *social life itself* something akin to progress-achieving methods of natural science. The basic task of social inquiry is to help humanity do this. Its task is the methodological or philosophical one of enabling people, groups of people, institutions and traditions, to put into social practice an appropriately generalised version of scientific rationality (responsible for scientific progress). What all this requires is that social inquiry be pursued as social methodology or social philosophy, concerned to help social life become more fruitfully rational, and not as social science at all.

In an attempt to take this last point into account, one might put forward what may be called:

The Revised Popperian Enlightenment Programme

A3. The progress-achieving method of science is the method of conjecture and refutation.

B3. This needs to be generalised to become *critical rationalism*, a general progress-achieving method of conjecture and criticism, trial and error. The basic task of social inquiry and the humanities is to help humanity build critical rationalism into social and institutional life, quite generally. The result of doing this would be the *open society*.[5]

---

4   My reasons for making this assertion are bound up with the conjectural essentialist conception of physical laws and theories that I have defended elsewhere (see Maxwell 1968, 1993a).

5   This revised Popperian Programme may be held to be implicit in much of Popper's great work (Popper 1969).

In *The Open Society and Its Enemies*, Popper in effect emphasises the fundamental importance of critical rationalism construed as a feature of social life – its close connection with liberalism, tolerance, democracy and the open society – and draws attention to often unrecognised enemies of the open society, most notably Plato and Marx, who, bewitched by false ideals of science or reason, or corrupted by the lust for power, try to establish totalitarianism under the guise of creating rational civilisation.

I am inclined to think that Popper's *The Open Society and Its Enemies* is *the* great work of philosophy of the twentieth century. It is nevertheless flawed by the conceptions of science and reason, upon which the whole argument of the book rests. As we have seen above, Popper's empiricist conjecture-and-refute conception of scientific method fails to solve the problem of induction. The above Revised Popperian Enlightenment Programme needs further revision, in that the key notion of scientific method needs to be improved. This leads to:

The New Enlightenment Programme

A4. The progress-achieving methods of science are those of aim-oriented empiricism, as indicated above and depicted in Figure 6.1. Science must conjecture that the universe is comprehensible in some way or other, a basic aim being to discover in what precise way it is comprehensible. At any stage science adopts a much more specific version of this aim, and seeks to improve this aim, and associated methods, with improving knowledge, within the framework of the fixed aim and fixed associated metamethods of aim-oriented empiricism. Because of the fundamentally problematic character of the basic aim of science, a range of rival, more and less specific aims (and associated methods) need to be developed and considered, in order to give science the best chance of developing a good specific aim, vital for scientific progress.

B4. Generalise aim-oriented empiricism, as depicted in Figure 6.1, so that it becomes *aim-oriented rationalism* (as we may call it), a general progress-achieving metamethodology which is applicable to any aim-pursuing human endeavour which has an inherently *problematic* aim. Level 5 now represents the basic aim of the endeavour (whatever it may be) specified in a sufficiently vague way to be unproblematic. As we descend from level 5 to levels 4 and 3, the one agreed, vague aim of level 5 splits into a number of rival, increasingly

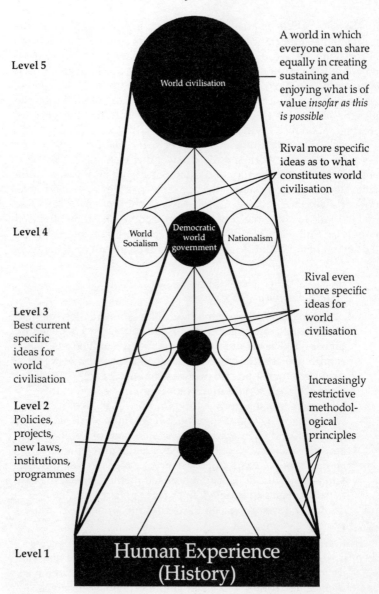

Level 5

World civilisation

A world in which
everyone can share
equally in creating
sustaining and
enjoying what is of
value *insofar as this
is possible*

Rival more specific
ideas as to what
constitutes world
civilisation

Level 4

World
Socialism

Democratic
world
government

Nationalism

Level 3
Best current
specific
ideas for
world
civilisation

Rival even
more specific
ideas for
world
civilisation

Level 2
Policies,
projects,
new laws,
institutions,
programmes

Increasingly
restrictive
methodol-
ogical
principles

Level 1

Human Experience
(History)

Figure 6.2: Aim-orientated rationalism

specific and problematic aims, with their associated methods, their associated trials, policies and programmes. At level 2, instead of *contributions to scientific knowledge* we have *personal, social and institutional actions*, considered from the standpoint of realising one or other aim. At level 1, we have *human experience*, that which is experienced as a result of level 2 actions being implemented, and in terms of which level 2 actions, and the policies and aims that they embody, are to be judged. All this needs to be applied to the endeavour of creating world civilisation, the *aim* here being profoundly problematic. The outcome, namely aim- oriented rationalistic efforts to create world civilisation, is indicated in Figure 6.2. (This is intended only to be a rough indication of the sort of thing aim-oriented rationalistic efforts to create world civilisation would be.) On this view, the fundamental task of social inquiry and the humanities is to help humanity put aim-oriented rationalism into practice in life, so that conflicts and problems may be resolved in increasingly just, peaceful, sustainable and cooperatively rational ways. What philosophy of science is to science (according to aim-oriented empiricism), namely a vital part of science itself concerned with exploring problems concerning aims-and-methods, so too social inquiry is to social life, namely a vital part of social life concerned to explore problems concerning what aims-and-methods to adopt in seeking to build civilisation.

This, then, is my proposal as to how humanity should set about learning from the solution to the first great problem of learning how to solve the second great problem, the problem of making progress towards world civilisation.

The New Enlightenment Programme, as set out above, differs from the Revised Popperian Programme only in beginning from an improved conception of science, aim-oriented empiricism instead of Popper's hypothetico-falsificationism. Note, however, that aim-oriented empiricism is a revised version of hypothetico-falsificationism; the former certainly includes the guessing and empirical testing of theories of the latter. Likewise, aim-oriented rationalism is a revised version of Popper's critical rationalism, and includes the guessing and criticising of critical rationalism. It is worth noting that aim-oriented rationalism, despite its name, is a kind of empiricism, a method for learning from experience. It differs from what empiricism ordinarily means, however, in that what is learned is in general *how* to do things of value, and experience is to be understood as human experience, what we acquire as we attempt to do things, partly succeeding and partly failing. The empirical method of science (aim-oriented empiricism) is a special case of the more general 'empirical method' of aim-oriented rationalism.

These last two versions of the Enlightenment Programme, (A3)+(B3) and (A4)+(B4), differ drastically from the first two versions of the Programme, indicated above, in that social inquiry is characterised in entirely different ways. For the first two versions of the Programme, social inquiry is social *science*, concerned to improve knowledge of social phenomena; for the second two versions of the Programme, social inquiry is social *methodology* or social *philosophy*, its relationship to social life being like that of philosophy of science to science (as depicted by aim-oriented empiricism at least).

My claim is that a kind of academic inquiry that is shaped by the attempt to put one or other of the last two Enlightenment Programmes into practice is intellectually more rigorous (other things being equal) than academic inquiry as we have it, by and large, at present, the outcome of the attempt to put one or other of the first two Programmes into practice. (This assumes, of course, that the basic aim of academic inquiry is to help promote civilisation by means of science and reason.) Here is my argument in support of this claim.

Granted that a basic aim of academic inquiry is, as the *philosophes* held, to help us achieve enlightenment, restricting academic inquiry to the pursuit of knowledge and technological know-how, as the first two Enlightenment Programmes above do, ensures that inquiry must be grossly irrational.

The notion of rationality that is being used here appeals to the idea that there is some (no doubt ill-defined) set of rules or strategies which, if implemented, give us our best chances, other things being equal, of solving our problems, realising our aims. Absolutely elementary rules of rational problem-solving (which ought to be accepted by all rationalists) are the following:

1. Articulate, and try to improve the articulation of, the problem to be solved.

2. Propose (or try out), and critically assess, possible solutions.

3. When necessary, break up the fundamental problem to be solved into a number of subordinate, specialised easier-to-solve problems.

4. Interconnect attempts to solve fundamental and specialised problems, so that the one may influence and be influenced by the other.

Academic inquiry restricted to solving problems of knowledge and technological know-how must inevitably violate three of these four elementary rules of rational problem-solving, granted that a basic aim of inquiry is to help us build a better world. The first two absolutely fundamental intellectual tasks of (1) articulating problems of living and (2) proposing and criticising possible solutions, possible human actions are excluded altogether from academic inquiry. Rule (3) is implemented splendidly, the whole mass of specialised academic research devoted to solving specialised problems of knowledge and technological know-how being the outcome of implementing this rule. But rule (4) cannot be implemented at all, owing to the non-implementation of rules (1) and (2).

By contrast, academic inquiry (judged from the standpoint of helping us create world civilisation) shaped by either one or other of the last two Enlightenment Programmes *puts all four rules of rational problem solving into practice.*

At this point it may be objected that we must first acquire knowledge before we can tackle problems of living. The first two Enlightenment Programmes, which recognise this, are thus more rational than the second two Programmes which in effect deny it – *despite* the above argument.

There are at least four things wrong with the claim that knowledge must first be acquired before problems of living can be tackled:

a. Many problems of living do not need new knowledge in order to be solved.

b. Even where new knowledge is needed, as in medicine perhaps or agriculture, it is always what new knowledge enables us to do that in the end solves the problem of living. What we primarily have to consider is our actions and their possible consequences, how conducive they are to solving our problems of living.

c. Unless we have some provisional ideas as to what our problems of living are, and what we might do about them, we cannot know what knowledge it is relevant to try to acquire.

d. In a very important sense, action is more fundamental than knowledge. We can only acquire knowledge if we can act more or less successfully in the world. Indeed, the very notion of knowledge only makes sense within the context of action.[6]

I conclude that social inquiry should not be construed to be social *science* at all, or even primarily the pursuit of knowledge: it is rather social *methodology* or social *philosophy*. When judged from the stand-

6   For a more detailed development of this argument see Maxwell (1984a pp.171–189).

point of helping humanity create world civilisation, it has the following three basic tasks:

a. to promote increasingly cooperatively rational resolutions of conflicts and problems of living, by cooperatively rational means

b. to promote aim-oriented rationalistic institutions and ways of life

c. to help enhance empathic, person-to-person understanding between people, essential for cooperatively rational action, but also of intrinsic value.

Social inquiry, construed in this way, *includes* the acquisition of knowledge of social phenomena; this is, however, rationally related to the intellectually more fundamental tasks (a), (b) and (c).

What emerges is a kind of inquiry that is a synthesis of traditional Rationalism and Romanticism. The former stressed the value of science, reason, truth, observation and experiment, objectivity, knowledge, technique; the latter stressed the value of art, imagination, emotional and motivational honesty, personal experience, subjectivity, insight, inspiration. Aim-oriented rationalism synthesises these clashing intellectual values into a new coherent whole.

Towards a kind of inquiry rationally designed to help us learn how to become civilised

In order to put right the mistakes of the *philosophes* of the eighteenth century, thus bringing into existence a New Enlightenment, new traditions and institutions of learning capable of resolving our second great problem of learning, changes need to be made to every branch and aspect of academic inquiry. These changes include the following:

1. There needs to be a change in the fundamental intellectual *aim* of inquiry, from the pursuit of knowledge and technological know-how to the pursuit of *wisdom* – wisdom being defined as the capacity to realise what is of value (and thus including knowledge, understanding and technological know-how).

2. There needs to be a change in the nature of academic *problems* – so that problems-of-living are included and are even regarded as intellectually more fundamental than problems of knowledge.

3. There needs to be a change in the nature of academic *ideas*, so that proposals-for-action, policies, philosophies of life are included as well as claims-to-knowledge.

4. What is meant by *intellectual progress* needs to change, from progress-in-knowledge to progress-in-ideas-relevant-to-achieving-a-cooperative-wise-world.

5. There needs to be a radical change in the whole nature of *social inquiry*. Economics, politics, sociology and so on are not sciences at all; their proper basic task is not even to improve knowledge. Rather their basic tasks are: (a) to promote increasingly cooperatively rational resolutions of problems and conflicts of living; (b) to promote the development of more aim-oriented rationalistic institutions and ways of life; and (c) to promote empathic understanding between people.

6. There needs to be a change in the nature of the *natural and technological sciences*. Instead of the intellectual domain of science consisting of just two parts – evidence and theory – it needs to consist of at least three parts: evidence, theory and research aims. Sustained discussion of problems concerning research aims must bring together scientific, metaphysical and evaluative considerations, in an attempt to discover the most desirable and realisable aims possible. Furthermore, scientific discussion must include some discussion of problems of living related to scientific and technological developments (as in, for example, the case of the involvement of modern physics in problems of defence and war).

7. There needs to be a dramatic change in the *priorities* of scientific and technological research – so that research aims are directed away from military research, away from research devoted exclusively to the interests of the wealthy and powerful, and towards the interests of those whose needs are the greatest, the millions of poor people living mostly in the third world.

8. There needs to be a dramatic change in the way *social inquiry and natural science are interrelated*. Instead of the natural sciences being pursued as if intellectually more fundamental, it needs to be the other way round. Social inquiry needs to be pursued as intellectually more fundamental – from the standpoint of the basic aim of tackling problems of living, of promoting wisdom.

9. There needs to be an even more dramatic change in the way the *academic enterprise as a whole is related to the rest of the human world*. Instead of being intellectually dissociated from the rest of society, academic inquiry needs to be constantly

learning from, speaking to and criticising the rest of society –
in such a way as to promote cooperative rationality and
social wisdom. Furthermore, it needs to be generally
recognised that the most important and fundamental
thinking going on in the world is the personal and social
thinking we engage in as we live, and which guides our
actions. All academic thought is but an outgrowth of this,
having as its basic purpose to help us improve our personal
thinking as we live. Academia needs to act as a sort of
peoples' civil service – doing openly for the public what
actual civil services are supposed to do in secret for
governments. Academia has the vital task of providing an
arena for the imaginative and critical exploration of aims,
ideals, values, ideas for the resolution of social problems and
conflicts – an arena which must exist if cooperative action is
to become a possibility in our vast, complex, rapidly
changing, conflict-ridden and unjust world.

10. There need to be fundamental changes in the role that
    *political and religious ideas, works of art, and expressions of our
    feelings, desires and values* have within rational inquiry.
    Instead of being excluded from inquiry, repressed, they need
    to be explicitly included and critically assessed, as possible
    indications and revelations of what is of value – and so that,
    through an interplay of mind and heart, we can come to
    have mindful hearts and heartfelt minds.

11. There needs to be a change in the aims, priorities and
    character of *pure science and scholarship*. Pure science (or
    natural philosophy) needs to be treated like music, literature
    or drama – esoteric and technical in some of its aspects, but
    at its most vital and important an integral part of life. What
    matters in the end is the personal knowledge and
    understanding that we seek, acquire and share with others
    as we live: expert, technical knowledge and understanding
    ought to be means to the growth of personal knowledge and
    understanding, active and alive in personal and social life.
    As Einstein once put it 'Knowledge exists in two forms –
    lifeless, stored in books, and alive in the consciousness of
    men. The second form of existence is after all the essential
    one; the first, indispensable as it may be, occupies only an
    inferior position' (Einstein 1973 p.80). Only a kind of inquiry
    that devotes itself rationally to the growth of wisdom in life
    can do justice to the vital personal and social dimension of
    pure science and scholarship. As a result of pursuing inquiry

in such a way that it is restricted to the acquisition of specialised knowledge and know-how, expert technical knowledge and understanding become dissociated from personal knowledge and understanding in life; they become ends in themselves, and cease to be means towards promoting growth of that essential form of knowledge and understanding 'alive in the consciousness of men'. A knowledgeable community of scientific and scholarly experts may result, but not a knowledgeable, curious, imaginative and self-critical human world.

12. There need to be dramatic changes throughout *education*. Thus, for example, seminars devoted to the cooperative, imaginative and critical exploration of problems of living need to be put at the heart of all education, from that of five-year-olds onwards.

13. There need to be changes in the way *mathematics* is understood, pursued and taught. Mathematics is not a branch of knowledge at all. Rather, it is concerned to develop, systematise and unify problem-solving methods, and to explore – to help us to see – problematic possibilities.

14 *History* needs to be pursued in such a way that it brings into contemporary reality an awareness of relevant past problems, and past successes and failures, in an attempt to aid the rational tackling of present problems.

15. *Literature* needs to be put close to the heart of rational inquiry, in that it explores imaginatively our most profound problems of living, and aids empathic, person-to-person understanding in life by enhancing our ability to enter imaginatively into the problems and lives of others.

16. *Psychology* needs to be pursued as an extension of literature, promoting empathic, person-to-person understanding in the real world – a kind of understanding that is so essential for cooperative action. If we cannot understand – enter imaginatively into – each others' problems, aims, hopes, fears, worlds, experiences, we cannot possibly act together cooperatively. This kind of person-to-person understanding – imaginative identification with others – is, indeed, I would argue, essential to our humanity, essential even to our consciousness, to our existence as persons. It is a great virtue of inquiry devoted to promoting wisdom that this kind of understanding is given an absolutely central place and role within inquiry (articulating problems of living being at the core of inquiry); and it is a great vice of inquiry restricted to

the pursuit of knowledge that it is almost entirely excluded from inquiry as unscientific, subjective, intuitive, emotional and personal. Psychology also, of course, has the task of explaining how our brains make it possible for us to have imaginative understanding of others, self-understanding, consciousness, an inner world.

17. Finally, *philosophy* needs to change so that it ceases to be a specialised discipline alongside other specialised disciplines, and becomes instead that aspect of inquiry as a whole which is concerned with our most general and fundamental problems – those problems which cut across all disciplinary boundaries. In the end there is just one basic problem for philosophy, and for inquiry as a whole: *How can we realise what is of value in this strange world in which we find ourselves?* All other problems of the sciences, humanities and life are specialised aspects of this basic problem – including the problem I have tackled here: How can we *learn* how to create an enlightened world? Philosophy, in short, needs to become again what it was for Socrates: the attempt to devote reason to the growth of wisdom in life.

I conclude that in order to bring into existence that which we so urgently need, a kind of inquiry rationally devoted to helping us learn how to become civilised, we need to bring about a major intellectual revolution in the aims and methods, the overall character, of the academic enterprise.

References

Berlin, I. (1979) *Against the Current*. London: The Hogarth Press.

Cassirer, E. (1951) *The Philosophy of the Enlightenment*. Princeton: Princeton University Press.

Einstein, A. (1973) *Ideas and Opinions*. London: Souvenir Press.

Gay, P. (1973) *The Enlightenment: An Interpretation*. London: Wildwood House.

Hayek, F. (1979) *The Counter-Revolution of Science*. Indianapolis: Liberty Press.

Maxwell, N. (1968) Can there be necessary connections between successive events?. *British Journal for the Philosophy of Science 19*, 1–25.

Maxwell, N. (1972) A critique of Popper's views on scientific method. *Philosophy of Science 39*, 131–152.

Maxwell, N. (1974) The rationality of scientific discovery. *Philosophy of Science 41*, 123–153 and 247–295.

Maxwell, N. (1976) *What's Wrong With Science?* Frome: Bran's Head Books.

Maxwell, N. (1977) Articulating the aims of science. *Nature, 265*, 2.

Maxwell, N. (1979) Induction, simplicity and scientific progress. *Scientia, 114,* 629–653.

Maxwell, N. (1980) Science, reason, knowledge and wisdom: A critique of specialism. *Inquiry, 23,* 19–81.

Maxwell, N. (1984a) *From Knowledge to Wisdom: A Revolution in the Aims and Methods of Science.* Oxford: Basil Blackwell.

Maxwell, N. (1984b) From knowledge to wisdom: Guiding choices in scientific research. *Bulletin of Science, Technology and Society 4,* 316–334.

Maxwell, N. (1985) From knowledge to wisdom: The need for an intellectual revolution. *Science, Technology and Society Newsletter 21,* 55–63.

Maxwell, N. (1986) The fate of the Enlightenment: Reply to Kekes. *Inquiry 29,* 79–82.

Maxwell, N. (1987) Wanted: a new way of thinking. *New Scientist 14,* May 63.

Maxwell, N. (1988) Reply to Bidon-Chanal. *Critique of Anthropology 8,* 109–112.

Maxwell, N. (1991) How can we build a better world?. In J. Mittelstrass (ed) *Einheit der Wissenschaften: Internationales Kolloquium der Akademie der Wissenschaften zu Berlin.* Berlin: Walter de Gruyter. pp.388–427.

Maxwell, N. (1992) What kind of inquiry can best help us create a good world?. *Science, Technology and Human Values 17,* 205–227.

Maxwell, N. (1993a) Induction and scientific realism: Einstein versus van Fraassen, Parts I, II and III. *The British Journal for the Philosophy of Science, 44,* 61–79, 81–101, 275–305.

Maxwell, N. (1993b) Can academic inquiry help humanity become civilised?. *Philosophy Today, 13,* 1–3.

Maxwell, N. (1994) *The Rationality of Scientific Discovery.* Cambridge: Cambridge University Press (forthcoming).

Popper, K. (1959) *The Logic of Scientific Discovery.* London: Hutchinson.

Popper, K. (1961) *The Poverty of Historicism.* London: Routledge and Kegan Paul.

Popper, K. (1963) *Conjectures and Refutations.* London: Routledge and Kegan Paul.

Popper, K. (1969) *The Open Society and Its Enemies.* London: Routledge and Kegan Paul.

Part III

Community Through Curriculum

Chapter 7

Levels of Discord

Roy Niblett

Two kinds of discord

Discord, whether in an academic community or outside it, can occur at many levels. It can be largely conscious or almost wholly unconscious. It is certainly possible for people to work together happily inside or outside an academic community on tasks (interesting or otherwise) that just have to be done – on washing up, planning a journey, teaching a technique, applying for a departmental grant, carrying out a piece of well-defined research – while disagreeing profoundly on the future development of society outside, or having political or religious convictions fiercely opposed to those held by some with whom they are at a more superficial level cooperating so well. As long as such longer term or deeper questions can be left on one side, the accord can continue, especially if some temporary crisis has to be resolved and motivation to tackle it is high. In such circumstances, the spirit of a whole community can stay vigorous even if there are real disagreements among its members.

In the university world, specialisation can itself be a source of accord to a team working in the same subject area if the climate around is encouraging. However, such accord can quickly deteriorate if funds dry up or if dictates from without, impersonal and un-understanding, lower morale.

If this is so within departments, it is certainly the case within universities as institutions. At a time earlier in the century when morale in places of higher education was far higher than now, when they were looking to a continuing future as autonomous bodies contributing – at least in their own judgement – to the social good, discords and disunity within them were a more temporary and less serious threat than they are now.

But now an impersonal state, with public opinion largely behind it, has come to demand that universities should be subject to its edicts: for the production of more and more graduates useful to it (with the state identifying the skills it must have); for a confining of researches

to those which promise a quick pay-off; for the introduction of
numerous managerial changes so that universities can be run more
economically and therefore 'efficiently'. A climate is generated in
which protest and discord are common, not so much because of the
changes demanded as because the academic community knows itself
to be vaguely at threat from without.

But the encroachment of the impersonal state challenges also at a
deeper level, pointing up a hidden conflict of purposes in the education a university gives. This conflict is only to be resolved if the
university finds the will and the courage to send a response that
draws very much upon first principles.

A university's concern must of course be with the advancement
of knowledge – hard knowledge gained by resolute exploration and
research. That, however, is not the only kind of knowledge needed
either by its students or society. If it succeeds merely in preparing
people for truths that can be objectively tested, leaving them to take
little account of those which can only be subjectively perceived, it will
fail an important part of its task.

Some kinds of evidence of what is true are of course provided by
facts and deductive logic. But other kinds can only be arrived at
personally and subjectively. Genuine knowledge that we love or are
loved is a personal perception; so is the knowledge that evil matters;
so too must the arrival be to us of beauty or of meaning in music. The
higher education on offer today tends to build into the minds of those
being educated pretty sharp limits to what is to be understood as
evidence. It may indeed be possible for it to avoid all matters other
than facts, theories and the acquisition of techniques. But to be
content consciously or unconsciously to pursue knowledge in this
dimension only involves a separation of life into sectors which are
potentially discordant. The long-term cost of doing so is high: for the
culture it generates will be thin and will tend to be nihilistic.

But how meet the challenge? It is not going to be easy, even if it is
possible, for an academic community to feel again how important it
is for students to reflect upon their own experience, to see again the
indispensability of knowledge which is essentially personal, moral
and subjectively acquired in addition to that which is objective and
open to proof.

There is, I am arguing, a fundamental discord between the idea
that universities should concentrate on teaching students to attend
only to evidence whose accuracy can be demonstrated and put to use,
and the idea that a university education also should so develop
people that they see the inadequacy of such a stance. Here is a discord
within the concept of a university's task which is more profound –
and more unconscious – even than the discord caused more directly

by the encroachment upon its autonomy of the power of an impersonal state. But the two are related: the dominance of the impersonal can only in the long run be countered by a revival of vision which is in its origin personal.

A look at the past

It may help if we look more closely into how the present state of discontent and of discord has arisen and become more threatening, and why the commitment of many university teachers has – often without their realising it – tended to become shallower. Thirty years ago in the UK, a committee under Lord Robbins was appointed by the Prime Minister of the day 'to review the whole pattern of higher education in Britain in the light of national needs and resources.' The far-ranging policies it recommended were informed by principles which were holistic. The chapter in the Robbins Report spelling some of them out is one which has no parallel in official reports on higher education later in the century. What was taught in places of higher education, it said, should 'promote the general powers of the mind'; higher education should transmit 'standards of citizenship' and should make itself responsible 'in partnership with the family for providing that background of culture and social habit upon which a healthy society depends' (Robbins 1963 para 28). It should never be forgotten, the Report went on, that 'education ministers intimately to ultimate ends in developing man's capacity to understand, to contemplate and to create...For the good society wants its citizens to become not merely good producers but also good men and women' (Robbins 1963 para 33).

We do not talk in such terms any more. The decade 1965–75 saw a great increase in the control a determined government was able to exert not only over the quantity but the nature and types of higher education to be provided. The times were becoming harder, money scarcer and the nation needed a far higher proportion of young intelligence relevantly trained. And, of course, it is obvious that the greater the proportion of the young having a period of higher education and the greater the tax burden involved, the stronger the argument becomes for allowing the state more control at least over numbers of entrants and over types and standards of qualification.

The changes in outlook manifest in places of higher education during the transition from 1965 to the present are certainly not to be understood, however, if they are regarded as wholly – perhaps even chiefly – due to economic pressures. A significant element in them has been a shift of values and perceptions in student consciousness;

and their expectations and hopes has come to influence the character and content of the higher education they were given more than it might have done in the more elitist first half of the century.

The widening social range from which students came, their aims and purposes in studying, and their lessened withdrawal from the world during their undergraduate years were among the factors making for a different experience of higher education from that obtained by their less numerous predecessors, even though entry standards were higher rather than lower. The growth of the habit of going away from their university or polytechnic on many weekends during term; the increase in ownership of cars and of travel in them; the co-educational schools from which the majority now came; the growth in the proportion of women students and closer relationships between the sexes; the far greater number of students living in lodgings; and cafeteria type feeding: these were all elements which made higher education a less segregated process than it had been. By the later sixties a greater proportion of students had less confidence in institutions or the powers that be than had their predecessors. It was not right, students held, that the university should be so merely impersonal in its apprehension of significances. In the UK, it had departed from its tradition of personal teaching. They saw the achievement of more equality – including that of the rights of students as against staff – as a moral issue.

But the lengths to which some of them began to take their protest against convention did much to punctuate public confidence in the universities and thus to play into the hands of the state (cf. for example Slipman 1991 pp.135–7, where there is a vivid description of the excesses of a student occupation at Leeds University). It helped to build into governments a greater determination that places of higher education should in future concentrate more intensively upon the production of specialists and practitioners of the hundred kinds their nations more and more needed. There remained in the mood of students, here and in many other countries, however, an underlying, inchoate disillusionment with contemporary society itself and the inadequacy of its values. That this was at a discord with their material ambitions went unrecognised. The criticism of American students of the Vietnamese war was in a large measure a moral one. The influence on the student outlook of existentialist philosophers, including Camus, but Marcuse too, was considerable. The threat of increasing depersonalisation seemed real. It was a threat voiced by Galileo in Brecht's eponymous play (trans. 1960) 'with time you may discover all that is to be discovered and your progress will only be a progression away from mankind. The gulf between you and them can one day become so great that your cry of jubilation over some new achievement may be answered by a universal cry of horror' (Brecht 1943 Scene 14).

The encroachment of the state

Recent years have seen a great intensification of the pressure from the government, with more and more emphasis laid on short-term rather than long-term objectives and fiercer stress placed on economic dividends. The prestige and the financial rewards which specialist attainments brought were moreover rapidly increasing. In Britain, the UGC, with such ability as still remained to it to act as a buffer between university interests and those of the government, ceased to exist altogether in 1989. It seemed by then to belong to a gentler age where dealings between the country and its universities were on a more personal basis, and Vice-Chancellors were not called upon to become Jarratt-like Chief Executives. Henceforward the responsibility for financing higher education and making it more 'cost effective' became that of two Funding Councils much more closely under the influence of the state and its requirements, which were in April 1992 made to coalesce.

What becomes clearer and clearer is that the agenda for the discussion of issues in higher education now is one the government itself has chosen. The promotion of 'the general powers of the mind' or developing 'the capacity to understand, to contemplate and to create' is not seriously to be attended to. The urgent questions include those of finance, student fees, loans, the possible introduction of a four-term year and shorter less expensive courses at least for first degrees, the provision of minimum hours which those employed (with tenure frowned upon) as lecturers should give to teaching, and plans for cooperating with industry so that higher education can in future aid national development more realistically.

Nowhere indeed, remarks Edward Foster (Acting President, Whitman College, Washington), does this dictation of the agenda for the debate seem more evident than in the question of the funding of research and development themselves. The range of solutions seems to have been predetermined. Absolute freedom will remain for the cheap (i.e. unimportant) disciplines, but technology, and science too (even nuclear physics), will often be on the leash of business and industry; the only thing to be resolved is how long the leash will be. In the background is a tacit acceptance of higher education as chiefly a means for manpower development and the creation of wealth.

The last decade has seen a rapid increase in the use of corporate management techniques, a process which, facilitated by computerisation, seems certain to continue. In universities as in many other institutions, decision-making about priorities has tended to shift to administrators, sometimes rather unnoticeably even to themselves. It may be significant that today only one or two among the hundred or so heads of universities in Britain are philosophers; most universities today rate very highly in their head his or her managerial skills and toughness. As in the country as a whole, so in institutions of higher education: policy directives, taken centrally by the state, affect and severely limit what can be done at the circumference – in individual universities, in their departments, even in the shape and content of the courses their departments offer. The academic community feels itself to be under attack. Today autonomy for institutions of higher education, though preserved, tends in practice to be more and more limited. Initiatives are encouraged only in authorised directions. Universities are aware that the range of reviews which the Funding Council undertakes – e.g. into the form of the academic year; into performance indicators; into the provision of continuing education; into strategic estate management – will be followed up by recommendations and advice, with financial sanctions available if it is rejected. In this climate, deeper questions relating to the purpose of higher education tend less often even to be asked. The managers – including civil servants and whether more remote or on the campus – are not for the most part interested in asking them. There isn't time anyway. Most university teachers, even if they had been inclined to ponder such questions, find themselves both lacking the necessary leisure and discouraged by the spirit of the age from indulging in so unprofitable an exercise.

A question avoided

In these circumstances it has become more and more difficult for higher education to think in terms of overriding purposes at all. Our society itself is rather lacking in purposes that can be called over-riding. We are all emotivists now, to employ the term used by Alasdair MacIntyre in his seminal *After Virtue* (1981). In it, he characterises the 'emotivist' as a person without ultimate moral criteria. 'Whatever criteria', he says, 'or principles or evaluative allegiances the emotivist self may profess they are to be construed as expressions of attitudes, preferences and choices which are themselves not governed by criterion, principle or value' (MacIntyre 1981 p.31). The individual, left with the freedom to choose but no hierarchy of values, is likely in his business or professional life to be a follower of its conventions and in his private life to lack any beliefs for which he would go to the stake.

But though we live in a world which fosters individualism it becomes harder for people to find any unifying meaning in things, or perhaps even to want to find one. The higher education on offer is not expected to help much in this matter and it can hardly be said that for most students it does.

The idea that education in a university can and will affect not merely technical advances in the world but also its moral climate is now scarcely envisaged. Adjusting a course to face economic, industrial or even environmental facts is one thing; questioning a culture of positivism with its focus on objectivity and a whole society which encourages emotivism is quite another.

Yet such fostering of detachment and self interest has widespread consequences. The West, powerfully reinforced by the technological and monetary rewards which following its example will bring, spreads its influence everywhere. Ours is an amoral world. Technology and professional expertise are instruments for the conquest and consolidation of power. Amoral multinational companies in manufacturing, telecommunications, transport, banking, and financial and insurance services are immensely influential today worldwide. Material prosperity and achievement fascinate. Such questions as, 'What is it all for?' and, 'What happens to human potentiality in the process?' are hardly glanced at.

In this kind of social climate, chances abound of escaping into an existence that lacks meaning altogether. Universities themselves are hardly less free from problems of drug addiction, alcoholism, sexual promiscuity and careerist ambition than the world outside. It is not easy to blot from the mind the television pictures showing serried ranks of intelligent, highly paid, young employees (some of them university graduates) in great factories of Japan spending their leisure time with eyes glued to pinball machines into which they insert coin after coin in competitive quest for a bigger harvest of ball-bearings than their fellows.

There are elements however much to be reckoned with in humanity which simply will not accept escapism as an ultimate stance. A whole dimension of truth seems somehow to have been left out. To assume that 'all moral judgements are nothing but expressions of preference' is close to declaring that all values and morals are forms of self-deception and self-interest. Standards of impartiality are invoked to show how admirable is our lack of standards of importance.

Higher education has in fact tended to become more and more instrumental in character and, even if it includes training in interpersonal skills, more and more subtly so. If its only significant aim is to produce and equip professionals to run with smoothness a managerial, electronic and consumer orientated society, what reason is there to think that such a society will take us in the long run where we really want to be? Contemporary society, left to itself, will set limits neither to its use of technology nor boundaries to growth except those which shortages of raw materials or skills arbitrarily compel. We cannot in the long run avoid more ultimate questions of objective. What is really meant by the term 'a better social future?' What does 'better' involve? And how do we find out? Even if we develop new and powerful types of control over the world that seem to be called for, that still leaves largely undecided the direction in which we want civilisation to go.

It is difficult to see what is to guarantee that a merely unconsidered future will necessarily be worth living in. The more that men or women go on simply using technological devices as ends in themselves or go on being hung up by them, the more the motive for living a life that has scope or depth is weakened. Why should clever animals who can calculate how their appetites can most deliciously be satisfied *want* to stay human?

A growing discord

It certainly cannot be said that most of our higher education now is conspicuously successful in producing more than a percentage of graduates who are 'all round' men and women: sensitively literate, numerate and civilised. There is of course no doubt whatever that the training of people with a capacity to analyse situations and high expertise of a variety of kinds is indispensable to modern life. But, by themselves, these are not enough. A widened and deepened awareness, and a sense of direction for human life, are also called for and places of higher education cannot leave to other institutions all the responsibility for educating them. What others anyway? The family? The churches? Big business? Schools? The political parties? The retort of course may be that it is the responsibility of individuals, not of institutions as such, and that many responsible people can be found in universities.

During the period 1970–1985, among the wide-ranging investigations into the state of higher education in any country was that sponsored in the US by the Carnegie Commission and chaired by Clark Kerr. It was action-oriented; not much concerned with how higher education could cope with a shifting moral climate and the need of society for orientation. In his realist *The Great Transformation in Higher Education (1960–1980)* (Kerr 1991), Kerr continues to reject as impracticable the policy that universities should make themselves more aware of the values to which the nation should hold and encourage their teachers to give more attention to the values hidden within the subjects they teach and particularly perhaps the way they teach them. That makes it the more significant that in 1989 Kerr published a powerful paper rejecting the idea that academics can any longer trade out of ethical issues by treating ethics simply as a matter of individual taste. Institutions of higher education ought in some vital ways to be 'the conscience of the nation', and university teachers must take their collegiate responsibilities seriously. Regrettably, university teachers, he says, have become 'more reluctant to serve on committees, more reluctant to make time readily available when they do, and more reluctant to accept the responsibilities of writing good reports on institutional matters. They wish to concentrate on their own affairs and not those of the institution' (Kerr 1989).

The situation in the 1990s, in the UK as well as the US, outside as well as inside the universities, is challenging. Threats caused by pollution, by the escalation of the world's population, by the certainty that genetic engineering involving human beings and the human species is going to be possible on a wider and wider scale – these need to be taken seriously by every intelligent man and woman. And they all impose not merely technical dilemmas but dilemmas for the conscience and the spirit, and not merely nationally but internationally. There is little evidence that universities are paying them more than intermittent attention. The sectional, departmentally confined, approach most common where there is interest at all is ludicrously inadequate to meet the challenge. It is not enough for the intelligent to be taught the techniques of architecture, engineering science, animal farming, computer theory, musical counterpoint, surgery, managerial science, anesthetics or economics, with such little encouragement given to the development of the aesthetic and moral insight needed to help them to realise the consequences of their knowledge.

The plotting of the future, if it is to serve mankind and not destroy it, requires many individual perceptions of what is worthwhile. It is not irrational to feel the importance of beauty, or of caring, or of life itself. In the long run, no subjectivity, no standards. Unless one knows for oneself, on the heart strings as it were, what a particular discovery made in the lab. may signify, that a particular line of Shakespeare has the truth of the matter in it, that a particular lesson taught in school by a student one is supervising is thrillingly good, one lacks criteria. People will of course depend greatly upon traditions of what to look at and what to value, acquired through their upbringing and education. Their insights, however, when they arrive at them, must be personal ones which need to be 'placed' – that is, brought up into consciousness and judged – if they are to matter more than transiently. An academic community which is to cohere in more than a

superficial way must trust the integrity, insights and standards of
many colleagues of whose subjects and specialisms one knows little
or nothing.

An approach to resolving the discord

Some of this trust, valuable though it is in bonding an academic
community together, can be of a token sort only. But if too much of it
is merely this the bonds are under threat. How today are more
members of an academic community to regain capacity to believe *at
depth* in anything at all and to be committed to their beliefs at a level
from which a new creativity can come – a creativity within the
academic community itself, indeed any community?

In the appreciation we rightly have for the integrity of the
scholar's and the scientist's knowledge and skills, we have lost sight
of the existence of another kind of disinterestedness. When Keats
declared himself to be 'certain of nothing but the holiness of the
heart's affections and the truth of imagination', was he not being in
a profound sense disinterested? Some kinds of truth can be discovered by analysis and research, others involve sources of authority that
are more inward. The tradition which looks for this second kind of
disinterestedness, not one based only on the evidence brought in by
the senses, has a long history. It goes back to Plato, Plotinus and
Augustine. Any perception of beauty which comes to us involves it.
Such experiences cannot of course be institutionalised, though the
community spirit of an institution can help them to arise. In essence,
they are personally realised and their attainment by one individual
is only even to be recognised by another if he or she too has had some
glimpse of the same encounter.

Some truths have authority because the evidence for them comes
from repeated observation or argued proof; there are others under-
written by the experiences and insights of sensitive, intelligent and
sane people over generations. And these can contribute depth to
those who have them. To recognise that Beethoven's symphonies are
great music is to acknowledge a truth that is not demonstrable by
logic. Aesthetic judgements must always involve an appeal to personal experience but they are not less rational because they do. We
have no choice but to draw upon reflection and introspection in
nearly every estimate we make of the relative value or the relative
importance of events in our lives. Genuine experiences of love,
bereavement, suffering, forgiveness, hope, are not simply self-con-
cerned; there is an element of disinterested truth about them. They
educate.

University teachers and research workers in many fields are dependent upon scientific method for their procedures and results and are tempted to deal only with a concept and range of 'truth' inapplicable to the making of value judgements. An understanding of human beings, their behaviour, their joys and sorrows, is left outside such knowledge. This is not at all to say that such reductionism is not legitimate in much scholarly work. It is indispensable if men and women are to arrive at right diagnoses and just verdicts in many situations. But such truth finding and truth telling is not the whole activity they are engaged in. And an academic community which shares nothing but truths of this kind lacks a dimension.

The admiration we can feel for integrity in friend or enemy, a realisation that cruelty to children or animals is wrong, a gift for entering deeply into the suffering of someone else – all have a strong element of disinterested truth about them. And this is so even though an element of self-pity or self-approval may be hovering, as an element of pride may hover in the heart of the scientist when his or her research produces just the result hoped for, or by mathematicians when their theorem 'comes out' and can now be triumphantly proved.

While the content of higher education must be closely related to students' professional needs, too narrow a concept within an academic community of what is relevant to those will certainly prevent the production of the kinds of professional the future will most need. There are many consequences of the rapid growth of opportunities for control over other people which the advancement of human knowledge and powers of communication are bringing about, as is our increasing ability to manipulate genes. The question of the concept, or norm, of the man or woman upon whom those controls are to be exercised will not go away. We have clues to the norm and how it is to be sustained in, for example, the expression of mind and desire in literature, music and art; in the concepts of human potentiality which have been seen and clarified in religious belief and in philosophic and religious exploration; in some of the medical and psychological discoveries of the past two centuries. But to follow these clues requires an active sensitivity and imagination, some sense of history, and a capacity to judge human nature informed by an experience gained at depth subjectively and interrelatedly from life and books and personal relationships. It requires that students shall not be specialists only but be able to estimate the relative importance of the factors, moral and spiritual as well as physical, which contribute to the answer. Only in this way will they be able to counter the threat inherent in going further and further ahead with small concern for the direction in which we are going.

A problem with most specialists is how to get them out of their protective shells. To a few it may be insoluble: some find it possible to show excitement easily within their specialist field, and very occasionally can be persuaded to reveal why it absorbs them. But if they are required to venture into wider questions – even, say, the place of their specialism in university education as a whole, or the moral or social consequences of research into it, or of applying its findings – they will declare that these are matters beyond their remit. The range of their social and moral responsibility, they feel, is limited. The claims of their subject are paramount and their subject is their proper territory. Other (less important) subjects perhaps may be able to 'take the strain'.

But this is to make oneself content with educating knowledge, and reason too, non-holistically. It enhances the discord. 'Whittling out pieces of the universe,' says Mary Hesse, 'which lend themselves to isolation, management and control in particular domains of phenomena suggests that all phenomena are similarly idealizable – that all problems are equally soluble. Hence the over-simplified "scientific" attempts to "solve problems" in, for example, the social and political domain, where the complexity of the environmental variables do not admit of such easy idealization' (Hesse 1985 p.108). Granted that there is a distinction between knowledge which is, as it were, external: between that concerned with facts, measurement and the apparent behaviour of things, and that which is more subjective and includes feeling and evaluating. Both kinds are indispensable. The kind of personal and moral commitment which is the mark of civilised people is not an irrationality.

How do we help students to recognise any authority other than from objective knowledge or logical reason? There is of course something absolute, something implacable in those, but to acknowledge no other authority is to be left with an existence at odds with life and with little direction in it. Much that is essential to all-round learning involves experiences which detached or technical study neatly avoids: personal suffering, personal happiness, the actual experience of cruelty, of good and evil, the mysterious, the tangle of human motives. To seek to educate people to be experts in a world that no longer has much meaning to it is a kind of madness and needs to be recognised as the madness it is. To rest content to cater only for the needs of our society as defined by an impersonal state is to produce a basic discord both in the individual and society – and to confine discourse to an area which is far too limited. An academic community functioning at this level only will be deficient in the moral resources and stamina essential to maintaining its health and its ability to give a lead – including a lead to the state itself. The most powerful community is one bound together by the shared individual insights and convictions of its members and the sense of purpose generated by them.

In our time, as George Steiner has said, there are luxuries of detachment one would like to afford but cannot (Steiner 1972 p.28) The direction in which we have been going in the last four decades, under financial pressures growing more and more severe, and governmental directives more and more compelling, may produce for us thousands and thousands of graduates able to solve technical problems disinterestedly and efficiently. But they may well regard larger questions which cannot be made into technical ones as if they were quite marginal. This is to leave the deepest hidden discord where it was. And such refusal to face reality can, I suggest, in the long run destroy not merely the university and higher education but, essentially, humankind itself.

References

Brecht, B. (1943) *Leben des Galilee*. (trans H. Brenton 1980 as *The Life of Galileo*. London: Methuen.)

Hesse, M. (1985) Reductionism in the sciences. In A. Peacocke (ed) *Reductionism in Academic Disciplines*. London: SRHE and NFER-Nelson.

Kerr, C. (1989) *Minerva*, Autumn, 139–156.

Kerr, C. (1991) *The Great Transformation in Higher Education (1960–1980)*. Albany NY: State University of New York Press.

MacIntyre, A. (1981) *After Virtue*. Indiana: University of Notre Dame Press.

Robbins, Lord (1963) *Higher Education* London: HMSO.

Slipman, S. (1991) In A. Gold (ed) *Edward Boyle: His Life by His Friends*. London: Macmillan.

Steiner, G. (1972) *Language and Silence*. London: Faber.

Chapter 8

The Power of Language

Marjorie Reeves

The myth of the Tower of Babel is uncannily prophetic. A mischievous god perceives a threat to his power in the cooperative aspiration of peoples to build a tower which would reach the heavens. So he comes down, scatters them and confuses their languages. Thus, already some primitive mind has recognised the connection between language and power and had grasped the principle 'divide and rule'. In the Christian liturgy, this ancient story from the Old Testament is often read at Pentacost, juxtaposed to a reading from the second chapter of Acts, when, in an international gathering, the Apostles were inspired to proclaim 'the wonderful works of God' in what became an explosive experience of languages, for everyone heard the same 'truth' in his own tongue. In this sharing of experience, a universal message was somehow coherently communicated across language barriers. These two stories encapsulate the paradox that language can be either a sharp divisive force or a powerful unifying agency in human experience. This paradox is everywhere apparent in the world today where language has assumed such a dominant role.

Words as weapons

Power and fear are closely linked. The psychological need for a secure base is an almost universal element in the human condition where craving for some kind of power and fear of the outside world go hand in hand. You dig 'fortifications' around your power base; on your ramparts you assemble your weaponry. Language has become a prime weapon in the psychological warfare which is now claiming a prominent place beside physical warfare. The astonishing range of language weapons today needs no emphasis: the communications explosion has multiplied them to a terrifying degree – terrifying in the sense that such weapons can destroy minds and spirits just as physical weapons destroy bodies. The ideologue, fortified in his own rightness, manipulates words into half-truths or untruths, repulsing any invading truth from outside. The propagandist handles his words without regard to any minted meaning, moved only by the overriding determination to convince. The tyrant fires off lies from his ramparts with one intent only – to kill opposition. Language used for domination is the very antithesis of language used as a vehicle for sharing truth.

There have, of course, always been battles of words and battles of books, but what confronts us now is a new situation. The media explosion has placed words as a tool of power-seeking in a key position in our culture. This in itself reduces their true currency value drastically. Regarded as a tool rather than as a vehicle of communication, the rules of the word-game today allow them to be battered into any shape which serves the ulterior purpose of the user. The bottom line of such a reductionist process is a devaluation of all speech and writing: words become merely subjective instruments, embodying only the prejudices and outlook of a particular culture, ideology or personal stance.

Academic 'territories'

By tradition, the academic use of words was supposed to be set above this enslavement to power-purposes. In a pure stratosphere of scholars, language should exist solely as an instrument for defining and communicating 'truth'. But the pressures operating in our society at large operate also in academia. Perhaps scholars, by virtue of their training, ought to be better equipped to detect the manipulation of language for ulterior ends, but, in fact, they are not immune from the temptation to secure their own power base in the field of knowledge and to fence it round by a special language. In an increasingly competitive world of scholarship, the question has to be asked: is language being used primarily as a vehicle for sharing new knowledge and insights as widely and generously as possible, or is it becoming increasingly a means of staking out a claim to a particular territory? Does a scholar write to share what he believes to be meaningful or to beat off rivals?

George Steiner has commented witheringly on the mass of mediocre jargon-writing poured out year by year simply to establish 'possession', and A.S. Byatt's novel *Possessions* has caricatured this academic possessiveness. Educationally, it has been argued that success is to be reached through mastering the 'code' of the relevant subculture or discipline and never confusing the languages of different disciplinary 'territories' (see Chapter 4). Discourse is to remain strictly within these limits, while any attempt to apply language and concepts across disciplinary boundaries is condemned as leading to disaster.

In a book on teaching students to be literate, the proponents of this advice give an example to illustrate their point. A student reading anthropology and English is commended for a paragraph in an anthropological essay because it uses 'the appropriate disciplinary concepts and language'. An English essay by the same student is condemned because anthropological ideas and perspectives intrude into what should be a strictly literary analysis. 'This student, we suggest, is disciplinarily confused. He is constantly being pulled away from strictly literary and dramatic issues to a larger social and anthropological perspective' (Taylor *et al.* 1988 pp. 15–16). So already in the educational process students are being taught that the way to win is by mastering a defined territory through its special language and never allowing oneself to pursue concepts in a broader language which takes them across boundaries into other fascinating territories – and what more fascinating excursion than an anthropological/literary one?

Literary criticism and 'meaning'

The study of text and speech in the context of their own cultures is, of course, a vital aspect of scholarship and has been for centuries. The assumption has traditionally been that the author's 'message' was worth listening to in its own authentic tones in great literature because, with understanding, it could be received across cultural barriers. In these last decades, however, the balance of importance has shifted from author to reader, speaker to listener. Each recipient, it is argued, creates his or her own text. Author's meaning has vanished behind reader's interpretation. A combination of factors seems to have brought us to this position. Influenced by scientific models, literary scholarship has shifted focus from the aesthetic to the analytic, from interpretation of meaning to dissection into 'parts'. Second, psychology has made us more sensitive to the subjective element in all utterances, especially those claiming to be 'truth-statements'. Third, open manipulation of language for propaganda purposes has engendered a widespread disbelief in the possibility that words can ever convey 'truth'. Fourth, we are witnessing a growth in relativism with regard to all belief systems. Could it be that a legitimate and important development in textual scholarship has been hijacked by a general shift in social attitudes?

The fact that what might be seen as a purely academic debate has entered the public arena suggests the answer Yes. The issue was highlighted by Peter Jenkins in the *Independent*:

In accordance with deconstructionist theories, the texts of the Western canon are seen as coded embodiments of the power structure of the society in which they were produced... Everything is relative, subjective, a matter of opinion. Pushed to its logical extreme, the perception drawn from such literary theory is that only those works which are 'politically correct', or culturally acceptable are worth attending to. (Jenkins 1991)

Again, Danah Zohar has described the present philosophical position thus: 'Philosophy must end its quest for objective universals because there is no "outside" platform on which to stand in looking for them. All platforms are inside some system of language or convention' (Zohar 1989). Whilst acknowledging that, in the past, philosophers have sought to strip away the illusions and misconceptions which blind us to some new or deeper truth, their aim was always to discover some better truth. Now, he asserts:

The end-of-philosophy thinkers claim there is no deep truth waiting to be discovered. In place of truth or reality, we have only limited human discourse, the systems of belief and acts of interpretation which each of us makes from within the prison of his own culture or language. Every value is equal to every other value, nothing is real or natural or authoritative, everything is up for interpretation.

The deconstructionists have been called a 'hermeneutic mafia'. Certainly the public perception is of conspirators who kidnap words and their meanings in some kind of secret game. A journalist's definition of deconstructionism runs: 'the critical method which kills off the author, freezes his text and then crushes any prospect of finding "meaning" in it' (Shone 1991).

Cultural doorkeepers?

Literary games are one thing; their educational impact is quite another matter. The underlying current of nihilism in this type of philosophical and literary thought can have a devastating effect on the growth of the next generation because it undercuts the very possibility of learning through the reception of new thought or meaning which may be surprising, uncomfortable, even shocking or belief- shattering. Anything unpalatable is to be thrown away. 'The truth, whatever is meant by that, if anything, is not the author's truth but the reader's, that is, *whatever it is comfortable and convenient for him to take from the text, if indeed, he finds anything acceptable*' (my italics) (cited by Culler 1983 p. 64). Using the metaphor of the mind as a room which we furnish, can we really assert that the doorkeeper of our cultural awareness only admits pieces of furniture which fit comfortably with the existing furnishings? Do we never take in a piece which upsets the whole arrangement? Going in the face of this, Karl Jaspers once pronounced that 'astonishment was the beginning of learning' (cited by Wyatt 1990 p. 50).

The key question, therefore, is whether we are so locked in our particular mind-sets that the possibility of real change, growth, 'conversion' in outlook through encounter with the 'other' is an illusion. The force of the cultural trap argument is real. Moreover, there is a sense in which we actually take refuge in it. 'Real presences' (in Steiner's striking phrase) are disturbing: 'we crave remission from direct encounter with the "real presence"... we seek the immunities of indirection... The secondary is our narcotic' (Steiner 1991 pp. 39, 49). But, he maintains, these narcotics are deadly: 'The mushrooming of semantic-critical jargon, the disputations between structuralists, post-structuralists, meta-structuralists and deconstructionists... all these carry within their bustling pretence the terms of more or less rapid decay' (p. 48).

How do we break out of the trap? Zohar concludes his article with the judgement that 'to get beyond it (i.e. "post-modern" thought) we would have to find some radically different grounding for objectivity.' Steiner, too, acknowledges the logical power, within its own parameters, of the deconstructionist position. He meets its challenge precisely by seeking to shift the ground of the debate. He argues: 'Current epistemology and certain directions in psychology... proclaim the vacancy of the subject... If the terms of the argument are solely those of immanence, the free real presence of meaning within form cannot be adequately defined or given metaphysical plausibility' (Steiner 1991 pp. 198–199). So Steiner postulates what he calls a 'quantum leap', or 'a wager on transcendence', that there is in 'the art-act and its reception... a presumption of meaning.' He acknowledges that such a belief 'cannot be logically, formally or evidentially proved... But let there be no mistake, such verification transcendence marks every essential aspect of human experience' (p. 214).

A wager on the power of language to communicate universal meaning

It is, indeed, the testimony of human experience which rises up against the extreme reductionist conclusion that there are no universal 'meanings' or 'messages' to be transmitted across cultural barriers. The power of language – all types of language – to change people finds innumerable witnesses in human history. 'Cultural doorkeepers' are certainly always on the alert, but great meanings can still crash their way in. If we look for the grounding of this fact of human experience, it must, I believe, be sought in the nature of human beings. Basic human experiences and the emotions they evoke, of birth, life and death, of love and hate, of good and evil, of tragedy and comedy, of security and adventure, do not change across time and place. They are archetypal experiences which speak across the generations and the continents. When these experiences in their basic elements are interpreted in 'great speech', they have great power. The adjective 'great' is, of course, here being used subjectively, but there is a kind of self-authentication which carries its own authority.

It is possible, perhaps, to distinguish between a more universal speech and a more culturally conditioned or immediate speech. Paul Ricoeur seems to be describing the first category when he writes thus about 'poetic language':

> My deepest conviction is that poetic language alone restores to us that participation in or belonging to an order of things that precedes our capacity to oppose ourselves to things taken as objects opposed to a subject. Hence the function of 'poetic dis-course' is to bring out this emergence of an in-depth structure of belonging to amid the ruins of descriptive discourse (cited in Hart 1991 p. 305).

At this point, the question arises: in what sense are we using the word 'language'? So far this chapter has been concerned almost wholly with the language of words, but, of course, 'language' today must cover a great variety of forms. Indeed, so it was from the beginning, for picture and sign languages preceded the languages of words which developed from them. Now, one might almost say that we have come full circle, for the sign languages of mathematics and the sciences occupy a position as central as the language of words on which in the past so much of our civilisation has been based. For the argument here there are two important questions. Do all these lan-guages – of signs, of visual images, of sounds, as well as words – have equal powers of universal communication to all sorts of people? Are all of them equally capable of communicating depths of human experience as well as technicalities of practical living?

In answer to the first question, it would seem at present that words are still the most universal medium and they remain so in education. This situation may be changing rapidly, both through the schools and through the influence of the media. Yet it remains true that, in the academic field, the whole range of the social sciences, as well, of course, as the humanities, still rely on words, even when they have recourse to sign languages as well. In general social intercourse, undoubtedly, words still maintain their pre-eminence as the most universal medium of communication.

The more fundamental question is: through what forms of 'speech' do the most deeply felt human experiences and desires best find expression? The speeches of pictures and sounds are possibly even more powerful communicators of basic human emotions than words. Whether through works of art or raw television images, through great symphonies or pop lyrics, through poetry or tabloid headlines, our imaginations are being continually awakened, even assailed, either in sophisticated or crude form. At the other end of the spectrum, pure thought, the realm of ideas, has traditionally been communicated most widely through word language. The beauty of a mathematical or scientific concept, expressed through an elegant formula, has spoken only to a privileged élite, but, again, this audience is widening today.

Between raw emotion and refined abstract thought lies the area of shared human experience, by which I mean here a fusion of thought and emotion in an interpretation which can be communicated. Here lies the most universal need for full and rich expression. Can 'human experience', thus defined, be communicated through scientific languages? Perhaps the question must be left open. But in the present stage of our culture it is still the case that mathematicians and scientists, for instance, need to share their 'experience', that is, the excitement and beauty of their discoveries, through words as well as pictures.

So the centrality of the languages of the arts, including words, still holds good as the sovereign media through which the broad range of human experience is shared. Yet the power and importance of all languages and the demands they make upon our sense of responsibility in the pursuit of truth-communication must be recognised and it may be that in the future communication in depth will take new forms.

Leaping the barriers

While accepting, then, that universal themes may be expressed in many languages, it is the power of great words to change their hearers which emerges in the following examples which I have chosen randomly from an innumerable crowd of witnesses. The first comes from my own experience in a seminar on Dante which I conducted in the University of California at Berkeley. I asked a student to prepare a summary of Dante's argument for the necessity of one universal ruler in the *Monarchia*. She arrived at the next class in a state of great agitation. 'I can't do it,' she said, 'I disagree with him so completely. His thought simply repels me.' We pursued our way through selected Dante texts and gradually she became more and more 'hooked', committed to understanding the nature of Dante's power. We moved too slowly for her growing excitement and as we neared the end of the course, she urged us to put in an extra session. 'I've got to get to Paradise,' she said.

Second, I recall a great dramatic occasion when the National Theatre put on the whole of the *Oresteia* in two lengthy parts. The house was packed and the audience response to these archaic themes of violence, blood-feud, revenge and reconciliation was almost palpable in its intensity. Of course, the translation was modernised in subtle ways to bring the experience within our own framework. But the essential archetypal themes, played back to ourselves, still made a mighty impact. It was a genuine cathartic experience.

Third, the power of great literature to transcend translation barriers has been debated innumerable times, but Eric Anderson, headmaster of Eton, supplies a truly surprising example of Sir Walter Scott in Chinese:

> A delightful Chinese told me recently that two new translations of *The Heart of Midlothian* had appeared in the same year and that other novels of Scott's were in hand. She herself had first read the Waverley novels in secret during her years as a peasant during the Cultural Revolution, when possession of a foreign book meant death. 'You see, we find in *Old Mortality* and *Woodstock* exactly what we went through in China,' she said, 'and... we recognise in Scott's peasants the Chinese peasants of today.'

'Thus we see,' comments Anderson, 'the power of great literature to leap the boundaries of time and space' (Anderson 1991, p. 46).

Masterpieces in translation pose the biggest question for the authenticity of communication. Gabriel Josipovice raised this in an article *Breaking the Language Barrier*. Of course he is aware of the traps in translation, both simple and subtle. (Among his simple examples he cites the amusing one of Scott-Moncrieff's 'hat shaped like a melon' for Proust's *chapeau melon* [bowler hat].) Certainly, he says, we read all literature, including that written in our own language, through the spectacles of our own culture. But does that mean that we are locked forever in our own cultural horizons?

Pushed to a logical extreme, 'our own culture' is not even the same as our neighbour's. 'Yet we all of us manage to get along more or less well with our neighbours and we know that the *greater our imaginative response to others, the more we will be able to understand them*' (Josipovice 1990). The words I have italicised give the key. It is readers primarily with 'imaginative empathy', says Josipovice, rather than those merely applying scholarship, who can best transcend the barriers of time and language and find the horizons of their own worlds enlarged by contact with those others. Here he makes a perceptive point. I argued above that it was the universality of the themes in great literature and art which broke the barriers. Josipovice makes a different point. Great writers, he suggests, 'transcend the horizons of their culture... in the sense of recognising the complexity and ambiguity inherent in all human motivations of all ages. Homer, Dante and Shakespeare are each rooted in a particular culture, but each transcends it in his portrayal of a grand but flawed human nature' (Josipovice 1990).

Four stages in 'reading the text'

Paradoxically, textual analysis, if used as an instrument for understanding rather than decomposing, can illuminate and enrich the message conveyed through the imagination,. As we attempt to engage in real dialogue with a 'text', Steiner's four stages in reading a text come to mind (cited by Barton 1988, pp. 62–63). First, there is an act of trust that there is something worthwhile to seek in it. Mysteriously, commitment to an intimation of 'worthness' comes before knowledge. Second, we explore it with our questions, seeking to get inside its cultural framework and domesticate ourselves within its unfamiliarity. Third, we bring it home and seek to 'naturalise' it within our own cultural system, playing its themes back to ourselves in our own language. Finally, we must 'give the text back to its author', recognising that the integrity of its life is independent of what we make of it. We are in some sense answerable for that integrity. It is this answerability, incidentally, which imposes on scholars and students an absolute prohibition against twisting the text for ulterior ends. Yet, in another sense, the message has now become our possession, assuming a form peculiar to ourselves.

Steiner had literary texts chiefly in mind, including the Bible, but in a broad sense his stages in 'reading' apply equally to all the visual arts and to music. The analysis of how Massaccio painted that desolating 'Adam and Eve expelled from Paradise' or Beethoven composed his grand Fifth Symphony opens up new dimensions in experiencing their message.

Language re-enthroned as the proper expression of humanity

Is the pendulum beginning to swing back the other way, that is, away from fragmented discourses pursued in tight little territories and back towards a renewed desire to share ideas and insights across conventional boundaries? There are signs that this is so. In the academic world there is a revival of interdisciplinary meetings. Seminars in which a scholar gives an exposition of his or her research to a broadly based audience of colleagues have sprung up. Or again, we meet seminars or open lectures on themes deliberately chosen to cut across disciplinary frontiers.

From an unexpected political quarter, outside the bounds of academia, comes strong support for the importance of communication as an essential attribute of human dignity. Why should anyone champion the political right to 'free speech' if they did not believe that men and women had important messages to get across to other people? Some academics may be playing language games, but around the world human beings are fighting for the right to speak. You do not risk torture or death for that right unless you believe that what you have to say has universal meaning beyond trivialities.

The connection between the political battle for freedom of speech and the academic debate about whether language can carry universal meaning emerged clearly in a series of lectures which Amnesty International arranged on 'Freedom and Interpretation'. Does critical interpretation necessarily undermine or devalue all speech of serious intent? One of the speakers, Jacques Derrida, faced this political challenge by arguing that deconstruction only aimed to improve concepts, not to destroy them and was hence no real threat to meaningful discourse. What the political context clearly brought home to the academics was that earnest men and women everywhere place a price upon language and communication far above the level where all utterance is perpetually being subverted, emptied of authentic meaning and made a prey to the continually shifting process of reinterpretation. A reporter on the conference, responding to the final speaker, Edward Said, concluded that one was left 'no longer doubting the power of communication or the ultimate belief in communication of even the most sophisticated of present-day critical minds.'

If that last statement is true, it is time we called the bluff of word-game players, not least in the cause of educational values. Great damage is done by totally destructive analysis which 'murders to dissect'. One of the powerful ways in which the young grow to maturity is by 'taking in guests' – whole guests, not dismembered limbs. For human beings live and move and have their being in communication with other people and with 'the other'. Among the many languages of relationships, the speeches of history, of ideas, of art forms, are crucial not only in intellectual growth but also in emotional and spiritual growth. To grow, we all need to give house-room to guests that knock at the door of our imagination. Steiner gives this metaphor a high overtone when he speaks of a 'terrible beauty or gravity breaking into the small house of our cautionary being' so that 'the house is no longer habitable in quite the same way as it was before' (Steiner 1991 p. 143). To put it more prosaically, continuing growth and vitality involve much furniture shifting as guests crowd in from all quarters and we lay the table for a rich feast of discourse.

Perverted language can assail the citadel of the spirit in wicked ways. It is all the more vital, therefore, that today academia should reaffirm its belief in, and its duty to nurture and guard, that aspiration towards true speech which is the life-blood, not only of the learned and learning community but of our whole society.

References

Anderson, E. (1991) *The Independent Magazine*, 17 August.

Barton, J. (1988) *People of the Book?* London: SPCK.

Culler, J. (1983) *On Deconstruction*. London: Routledge and Kegan Paul.

Hart, K. (1991) The poetics of the negative. In S. Prickett (ed.) *Reading the Text. Biblical Criticism and Literary Theory*. Oxford: Blackwell.

Jenkins, P. (1991) The follies of the politically correct. *The Independent*, 8 May.

Josipovice, G. (1990) Breaking the language barriers. *The Independent*, 30 June.

Shone, T. (1991) Unmasking de Mann who knew too much. *The Independent*, 26 October.

Steiner, G. (1991) *Real Presences. Is there anything in what we say?* London: Faber & Faber.

Taylor, G. *et al* (1988) *Literacy by Degrees*. Milton Keynes: SRHE and Open University Press.

Wyatt, J. (1990) *Commitment to Higher Education*. Buckingham: SRHE and Open University Press.

Zohar, D. (1989) A wonderland without the wonder. *The Independent*, 19 December.

Chapter 9

Transferring Learning in Higher Education
Problems and Possibilities

Anne Griffin

Introduction

In our search for what is common and shareable in an academic community there lies at the heart of the curriculum an intriguing and elusive idea: the idea of transferable and generic skills, abilities or, so as not to beg the question at the outset as to *what* might transfer, let us say: 'elements'. The idea of transferability appears in both vocational and general education contexts: in the former, mainly in further education literature; in the latter, in discussions within philosophy of education about the idea of general thinking skills, or abilities, or 'general powers of the mind' (Robbins 1963 p.6 para 26).

What has and has not been established in this area is complex, for transferability raises fundamental questions about the nature of training and skills in relation to education, of the integration of knowledge, of mind and of personality. These are questions I cannot address here, since my aim is to draw out some key issues from the philosophical debate on transfer, which are relevant to the search for increasing commonality and cohesion in higher education. Higher education is concerned to promote both the general personal intellectual development of students, as well as their specialised professional development, and I shall draw on the philosophical literature on both vocational and general education to support my argument.

After discussing some key definitions of transferability I shall first, consider the transfer of technical skills and abilities, and of attitudes and motives in vocational education. Next, I shall discuss the central question of general powers of the mind. Third, I shall assess the claims of problem-solving in achieving transfer. Fourth, the central role of teaching processes in promoting or obstructing transfer will be considered. I shall then, penultimately, discuss the role of attitudes, dispositions and character-traits in promoting transfer. Finally, I shall draw some lessons for higher education from transfer in the arts.

The meaning and value of transferability

The idea of transferability has the same aura of untouchability as that enjoyed by 'integration' since the 1960s (Pring 1971). That transfer takes place was and is so powerful an assumption as to be deemed beyond discussion: what we think or can do just *does* transfer from one situation to another. Indeed, there is a similarity and overlap between the concepts of integration and transfer which I can only touch on here. We hope to 'integrate' our personalities to avoid fragmentation: this is partly to transfer – something – from one context (one part of our mental equipment, here) to another. Just as we sense that we integrate our ideas, feelings and actions – when we are not alternatively conscious of the fragmenting or compartmental-ising influences in daily life – so with transferability we are confident that it must somehow happen:

> Yet there *must* be transfer or something in its place, for our whole hope of making sense of the world around us consists in studying restricted samples of it in a compressed form, and then expecting the rest to make sense one way or another. (Perry 1972)

Perry's contribution to this topic remains important, though it is little mentioned in current discussions. He notes that perhaps the largest and most frequently made transfer claim relates to the transfer of attitudes and principles, there also being cognitive elements in each kind of transfer he discusses. To be an educated person necessarily implies that much more than cognitive transfer has taken place in schooling:

> So alongside the cognitive transfer, we must be assured that attitudes, dispositions, principles, forming rules, motivation also perhaps, can exhibit the quality of turning up in situations lying years ahead of school, and undreamt of at the time of one's education. (Perry 1972 p.23)

But the trouble is, as Perry says, despite the plausibility of this hope transfer simply fails to appear in large numbers of cases. In reviewing meanings of transfer, he comments that 'our stock looks rather like a heap of objects on a coster-monger's barrow – flung in from all sides to try and explain the problems arising in education.'

The basic notion that we transfer some element of learning from one place to another can refer to the following (he says non-exhaustive) list:

1. a technical and philosophically trivial use of transfer in learning theory
2. transfer in a cognitive sense
3. transfer as the practical utilizing for other ends of knowledge gained elsewhere (as with training)
4. transfer as the idea of applying pure knowledge to other areas(... a study of pure mathematics gives us an advantage in all applied areas, e.g. statistics, computing, spherical trigonometry)
5. transfer in a sense penumbral to or clustering round cognition, of attitudes, dispositions and feelings
6. transfer of principles, large generalisations, rules and so on (Perry 1972 p.23).

In what follows particular attention will be given to Perry's senses (2), (3) and (5). In one sense, all transfer *must* have a cognitive element (in that skills, attitudes, dispositions and feelings have such): thus sense (2) is a common element throughout this chapter. Sense (5), the transfer of attitudes dispositions, feelings (to which we might add motives), is perhaps the most interesting and certainly the most difficult area of transfer to explore, and my discussion will give it prominence.

I omit sense (1) which virtually equates learning with transfer: we use what we learn in whatever contexts; sense (4) I take to be *relatively* unproblematic (though how and to what precise extent such transfer occurs is not clearly established, and the boundaries of its application remains disputable). Sense (6) overlaps with both cognitive and attitudinal transfer and belongs with discussion of both. Sense (3) most closely refers to transfer of job skills, and to this I now turn.

Transferability in vocational education

That skills, abilities and indeed attitudes, *do* transfer is largely taken as read in the literature on vocational education from the 1970s onwards. The Training Services Agency in one of its earliest documents (TSA 1975) makes that assumption, and its parent body the Manpower Services Commission rarely considers the notion to be problematic: one exception is in a research paper, written, we must note, by critics of transfer Annett and Sparrow who are careful to state that their views do not necessarily reflect the views of the MSC: 'First, there is no easy way which enables us to say with any degree of confidence just how much any given achievement or skill will *transfer* (their emphasis) to any other' (MSC 1985 p.10, Annett and Sparrow 1985).

I cannot trace here the subsequent adoption and development of the transferability assumption in 16–19 education and training literature, for instance in both the documentation of the National Council for Vocational Qualifications (NCVQ), which has the remit to distinguish levels of competent performance in employment, and in the work of the Business and Technician Council (BTEC) which gives transferability the same unquestioned status. Certainly if transfer did work in vocational areas, then immense benefits would accrue: the employee would be protected against being trapped in a local skill which became obsolete; trainers, too, could be confident that they were providing a flexible, adaptable and relevant training which maximised the employment possibilities of their trainees.

Lack of transfer in the skills area

But there are fundamental problems of meaning and coherence with transfer in this technical sense. The early psychological experimental work of Thorndike assumed that transfer was an empirical matter only but, as Perry argues (Perry 1972 p.21), how does one establish from the learner's behaviour that it was the *transferred* element (if, indeed, anything was *transferred*) which influences his or her behaviour in new contexts of learning? Correlation of abilities between two areas might just as well be explained by the presence of an interest or attitude. R.F. Dearden cites Pirsig's *Zen and the Art of Motorcycle Maintenance* where Pirsig suggested that a certain Zen state of mind was a condition of general technical competence but, as Dearden adds: 'that is not an ability; it is a condition in which abilities may most profitably be exercised' (Dearden 1980 p.283). For instance, a pupil who excels in various map-reading skills such as estimating height and slope and following grid-references does not necessarily have a general map-reading skill. An intense map-reading interest may make him or her eagerly learn each separate and specific task of map-reading. (Or, a lathe-operator may have a specific skill, as Dearden notes in a further contribution to the topic (Dearden 1984 p.60), which might *appear* to transfer, since there are many lathe-operating firms, and thus many identical contexts for its application. This is the trivial use of transfer – Perry's sense (1) – but its use is nonetheless widespread in common discussion.)

How, as Perry asks (Perry 1972 p.21), is an 'element' in a learning situation to be characterised, identified, isolated and transferred? How, in other words, does one recognise the *relevant* respect in which two activities are similar, avoiding a lowest common denominator of similarity? (An apocryphal story claims that it was earnestly discovered that the same finger movements are used in packing cheese in boxes as in playing the piano!) The central point is that concrete technical skills *cannot* logically transfer for skills are specific to a context: a skill is attached to a body of knowledge belonging to (here) a particular occupational area. And the more concrete a skill, *the shorter its useful working life.*

Broader transfer possibilities in vocational education

If there is no transfer of knowledge and skills in the vocational technical area, either because skills are complex and specialised or that they transfer only at a trivial or meaningless level, is there any sense in which the transfer of attitudes and dispositions *especially relevant to a vocational context* may both have potential application and be of educational value?

It is generally recognised that work of a non-alienated character can provide central meaning in human life: Conrad, for instance claims (Conrad 1902) that work gives you the chance to find yourself, to discover what you can do and extend your boundaries. Such a view of the potential value of work indicates that *motives* are deeply pertinent to the development of personal identity, and that vocational education has thus an intrinsic as well as an extrinsic value. Dewey's broad definition of vocation as a direction of life activities significant to a person is relevant here: he believes that we are disabled socially as well as personally without work, which he defines as extending beyond employment to encompass all life contexts calling for our intelligent and effective action. A calling (vocation) is an organising principle for knowledge and intellectual growth, 'a magnet to attract and a glue to hold' (Dewey 1916 ch.23).

Vocational education thus seen (and considered, for our purposes, within an educational institution) could be a rich source not only for intellectual development, but of the attitudes and values relevant to a more positively conceived and experienced working life. Bridges too has recently, if not unproblematically, advocated the values of enterprise (Bridges 1992). Integrity, responsibility or perseverance, for instance, might be promoted by the 'magnet or glue' motivation Dewey mentions. To achieve some balance between aesthetic, technical and business constraints in a degree course project in design may require restraint, maturity and courage in working out how far to press, modify or jettison one's original work conception in the face of outside or tutor pressures. Personal development, while often ill-defined or not at all defined (though see Peters 1972 and Pring 1984) is a much vaunted aim of *vocational* courses at all levels of education. The cognitive, emotional and attitudinal processes undergone by the design student in the above example could surely, for instance, contribute to personal development in an educationally appropriate way.

Preoccupation with the (mainly wrong) assumption that transfer is present in technical areas has obscured the fact that vocational education *can* be seen as centrally concerned with the development of such attitudes and dispositions: the extent to which these may transfer will be discussed below.

Are there general powers of the mind?

When it comes to gauging transfer possibilities in non-vocational education, the discussion is typically cast in the form of inquiring whether there are general powers of the mind, or general mental skills and abilities. Since the 1960s, this has been debated at intervals within philosophy of education, most notably in Paul Hirst's influential paper (Hirst 1965). The argument itself, however, is as old as Plato, and has been conducted since by Locke, and most notably as far as university education is concerned by Newman. To Newman cultivating the intellect meant: 'a faculty of entering with comparative ease into any subject of thought and of taking up with aptitude any science or profession' (Newman 1873 preface).

In what follows, I shall try and assess the progress of this debate but it is first necessary to look at the idea of general education itself. Charles Bailey (Bailey 1984) argued that *liberal* education (and in the current context distinctions between liberal and general education are not relevant) must provide knowledge and understanding of a fundamental kind in order to *ensure* (my emphasis) a generality of application over different contexts:

> Principles are more fundamental than the particulars submerged under them though the principles may in some cases have to be arrived at by a study of particular cases; and these general clusters of rules and principles which we refer to as disciplines are more fundamental than any isolated facts or items of knowledge unrelated to anything else. (Bailey 1984 p.23)

Bailey later neatly turns the utility argument on its head by arguing that a liberal education is *practical* and *useful* in contributing to a wider understanding that helps develop reason and independence which cannot become obsolete.

I cannot pursue here the separate and problematic issue of whether the principles Bailey refers to above need to remain instantiated in *disciplines*, but what is important here (and it is a widely held view) is the claim that *generality* of knowledge, grounded in principles and rules, provides a potent basis for transfer.

Principles which are designed to apply to instances will, of course, transfer across numerous examples of the *same* instance (transfer in trivial sense (1) again). What is necessary is to show how bodies of knowledge and understanding (whether organised strictly in disciplines or by virtue of some other classification) play a significant part in transfer, a view stoutly maintained as I shall show below.

One might argue that this question is undercut by what I might call the 'accretionist' argument: the broader and deeper one's repertoire of knowledge and understanding is, the more life situations, theories and practices have *thereby* been covered. Nothing is being *transferred*: it is merely that one's quiver is richly stocked, and that one is in possession of a relevant principle, skill or area of understanding to draw on from that store, as the need arises. That comprehensive knowledge acquisition must always be a severely limited achievement does not affect the point that transfer is often claimed to be at work, when drawing on a wide knowledge base is in fact meant.

A central argument in the case against vocational transfer was that skills are context-specific. Similarly there is a powerfully-held view apropos general education that no general thinking ability exists independent of a precise (often disciplinary) body of knowledge, rules and principles. Hirst gave this view elegant prominence (Hirst 1965) and it has found broad sympathy since with a variety of thinkers including Barrow (who now holds it more strongly than Hirst himself does) and, with more sympathetic qualifications, by Dearden.

Taking Dearden's position as representative, since he advances the argument furthest (Dearden 1980), the point would be, for instance, that the exercise of imagination in one area (for example, science) does not itself confer the capacity to exercise it in another (for example, poetry): imagination cannot transfer *per se*, unattached to the specialist body of knowledge that is its source. Dearden goes on to note that there is an element common to all instances of good judgement, that is getting something right in difficult circumstances, but that very different and specific accomplishments are involved, excellence in which requires specific knowledge (Dearden 1980 p.284).

It is in the acknowledgement of *some possible* commonality that Dearden makes a helpful suggestion (which has been picked up by later writers such as Andrews and Bridges – see below): to see the reed-warbler, the constellation of Orion or the symptoms of pneumonia will require specific abilities and knowledge, but there still can be something *general* in all the variety of cases even if it is only the general power of focusing our visual attention. Showing specifics to be necessary (as Hirst does) does not force us to conclude that the general is impossible. Dearden concludes that we need to proceed on a case by case basis, by reflecting on the possible learning content of such a skill or ability (and indeed, context, as I shall discuss below). There is nothing, then, *conceptually* impossible about general powers of the mind.

It might, finally, be urged that to discuss general powers of the mind necessitates a critique of 'critical thinking' as a subject which is taught, and as a movement which is widely under scrutiny. The extensive literature on critical thinking shows that the concept is hotly contested both in terms of meaning and coherence, and I take the view that general powers of the mind can be profitably discussed independent of 'critical thinking', as I have done here.

Problem-solving: a favourite candidate for transfer

It is worth considering Dearden's more educationally interesting example of possible transferability: that of problem-solving. Problem-solving in this world of all-pervasive and intractable problems is habitually championed, in all imaginable contexts, including both vocational and general education, as a key instance of the success of transferability. Here the argument is then not that general abilities are sufficient for some task, but that they are *possible*, and may have valuable contributions to make. Dearden prescribes a set of general rules and tactics relevant to solving a wide range of problems not confined to a single subject or discipline:

> A person with general problem-solving ability might have learned how to employ the following rules or tactics with skill: pick out essentials; discriminate between what is relevant and what is irrelevant; identify assumptions and consider their acceptability; look for analogous problems the solution to which is already known; refrain from being critical of emerging suggestions too early; try a different way of looking at the problem, or re-define it in a different way. (Dearden 1980 p.285)

Lists telling us what problem-solving supposedly involves proliferate in educational literature, but an interesting feature of Dearden's discerning suggestions is that beyond the undeniable degree of knowledge and skill required in the exercise of such an ability, attitudes, values and character traits are called into operation too. Discriminating between what is relevant or irrelevant, for instance, is to distinguish what matters – what is useful or meaningful – from what does not. Refraining from early criticism takes restraint and generosity; looking at a problem differently may take courage in modifying or relinquishing a favourite view; and so on. It is clear that more than knowledge is required to accomplish problem-solving. But even if problem-solving involves more capacities than are usually recognised, and even if we accept that Dearden's suggestions can outline further possibilities for its success, I would want to argue that its prominence as a central concept characterising how a learner should focus on his or her subject matter, or task, or course of action, should not go unchallenged. The value and scope of 'problem-solving' itself should be seen as problematic.

We identify problems in the light of principles, beliefs, attitudes and motives, and these may be prompted or developed by the way we confront what R.S. Peters called the general conditions of human life (Peters 1977):

> What is he to make of objects in the natural world...of other people and their reactions to him and to each other... In what way is he to react to authority, suffering and violence... what *attitudes is he to take towards the cycle of birth, marriage and death...*

These are questions arising from the general conditions of human life. The kind of understanding achieved through confronting such predicaments is understanding to which (I would accept) the disciplines of knowledge can contribute insights. But the phrase 'knowledge for its own sake' is too abstract to define such understanding; nor may this knowledge be useful in the immediate practical sense. But it may be useful in the sense of being broadly meaningful, and thus be both profoundly and practically for *our* own sakes. This broader thinking and questioning mode cannot be fully characterised as problem-solving with its positivistic (where not strictly quantifiable) connotations, and the further implication that solutions are in principle possible, if neither obvious or imminent. The understanding we achieve from confronting the general conditions of human life comprises not only knowledge but attitudes, dispositions and values which may provide us with important if not yet clearly delineated transfer possibilities.

Dearden's argument that *some* generality has not been proved impossible is carried further by Andrews (Andrews 1990 p.73) who points out that if thinking is always thinking about something specific (some object, activity, task, topic, subject matter, etc.), it is crucial to clarify what the criteria for the application of the term 'specific' are. If thinking is to be 'domain-specific' (as Hirst and Barrow would

argue) then we need a supporting theory of domains, and this does
not unproblematically exist.

We can as Bridges (Bridges 1992, 1993) notes, draw and redraw
boundaries of cognitive domains to serve our varying chosen purposes, and there may be a variety of logical and conceptual distinctions between different kinds of knowledge which could reveal a
variety of interconnections capable of providing further channels for
developing understanding and skill between domains. Pring gave us
some helpful clues about how to proceed when he analysed different
types of connections between disciplines: for instance, that mathematical propositions are *essential* to various kinds of scientific enquiry, that some empirical understanding might be *relevant* to
different types of aesthetic appreciation (without some knowledge of
human nature one could not judge a fictional character to be 'true to
life'); or that psychological judgements about a person's state of mind
may be *necessary conditions* for making moral judgements about that
person (Pring 1971 pp.196–199). Pring's suggestions have not, to my
knowledge, been followed up by a mapping-out investigation which
is only partly empirical. Such work might establish 'that there are
thinking skills necessary to the successful solution of some problems
located in different domains' (Andrews 1990 p.77) – a possibility
ruled out by Hirst and Barrow.

The role of teaching processes in transfer

If the elucidation of transfer possibilities needs further research as
suggested above, I now want to argue that there is work too for the
teacher to do *within the teaching process* in promoting transfer in both
vocational and general areas. I would argue that a teacher has the
responsibility to plan deliberately for possible transfer (not merely
'facilitate'). Perry points out that 'we have a choice of aims and can
budget for the transfer situation we want' (Perry 1972 p.24). A
teacher's approach may promote a limited transfer as with training,
or by providing an understanding which the student is yet unable to
put into practice. It may also obstruct or arrest transfer by failing to
promote possible conceptual connections in any subject-matter, or by
not showing how such connections may readily be applied. (Dearden
too mentions contexts of educational failure where a teacher failed to
point out a potentially general application of something taught, thus
preventing legitimate transfer (Dearden 1980 p.283).)

There are complications of both a logical and moral kind for a
teacher here. Transfer requires, first, the intellectual *grasp* of transfer
potential within any given subject matter. Second, transfer requires

diligence and perseverance in its pursuit. Third, it requires an appreciation of the significance of the transfer under scrutiny for the learner. All of these requirements are inadequately recognised.

Do such requirements need to be met in face-to-face interaction between teacher and learner? It is an empirical matter whether a given learner will grasp transfer opportunities better thus, but to the extent to which transfer discussion *is* desirable, this is in tension with certain current versions of learner-centredness. Reductions in class-contact time, a move which the pressure of diminishing resources encourages, can be presented under the guise of the more respectable sounding 'taking responsibility for one's own learning'. It is of course of the first importance to promote such responsibility in the interests of a student's autonomous self-development, as, for instance, in the Open University model of learning. But tutorial, counselling and residential support underpin a student's self-directed effort: it cannot be all 'do it yourself'.

Transfer of attitudes, dispositions, feelings and motivations

Attitudes, dispositions, feelings and motivations are all major candidates for transfer. (Each of them has a cognitive dimension too, as argued above.) But, as Perry warns (Perry 1972 p.23), there is extensive evidence both for *and* against such transfer. We cannot identify even a tentative disciplinary base for attitudes and the like to belong to, for there is no such thing as a theory of social domains. As Bridges rightly states:

> An empirical mapping of the social system of knowledge will display infinite numbers of interconnections in a way which no current theory of domains portrays. (Bridges 1993)

Attitudes such as confidence, openness to collaboration, interpersonal abilities and skills would need investigation across a range of contexts in general and vocational education.

A different kind of procedure to the mapping exercise just mentioned is required when it comes to considering whether character traits are transferable. This, I think, is a fruitful line of enquiry. Passmore, for instance, refers to critical thinking as a character trait (Passmore 1967). One should not, he says, merely criticise a level of achievement *within* certain kinds of specialist or technical performances. It is necessary to consider more broadly the value of a type of performance itself (for instance, of the value of executions, as distinct from producing more highly skilled executioners):

> A critical person, in this sense must possess initiative, independence, courage, imagination, of a kind which may be com-

pletely absent in, let us say, the skilful critic of the performance of a laboratory technician. (Passmore 1967 p.198)

Courage, for instance, may be necessary to criticise prevailing social values of a narrow kind; so too with imagination (in Mary Warnock's definition), in seeing possibilities beyond the immediate, and being open to the incorporation of such possibilities within one's future plans. A critical spirit, Passmore argues, which involves being ready and willing to produce relevant grounds to defend what one says, transcends mere professional competence as a critic of techniques. R.K. Elliott's analysis of what he claims is involved in achieving an excellent understanding of a complex and interesting topic develops this idea of traits considerably further (Elliott 1975). He claims that in such an endeavour we *typically exhibit* (my emphasis):

1. certain moral or quasi-moral traits such as integrity, lucidity and courage, which he calls intellectual conscience

2. certain psychical powers such as involvement, ambition, adventurousness, tenacity, endurance, hope and faith, which he calls intellectual eros: 'a composite of energy and desire which calls them into play for the sake of achieving understanding.' Added to the necessary skills and knowledge demanded by each context, these may be exercised in (for instance) retention and anticipation, synthesis and synopsis, in pushing ideas to their limits, and in weighing pros and cons and sensing the balance.

Integrity and courage, for instance, might be brought into play in ensuring we are sceptical where there is inadequate evidence, and willing to accept the force of relevant reasons when it is uncomfortable or even dangerous to us to change our minds. *All* of Elliott's 'eros' characteristics (and some others!) might be instanced in the work and behaviour of those scientists who discovered the structure of DNA. Some may be instanced in the still vital, if more modest, attempts of a student in maintaining the hope and enthusiasm involved in seeking out little-known sources in pursuit of a theory or idea he or she is drawn to.

If this characterisation of intellectual *conscience* is uncontroversial and if the idea of psychical powers has at the least a suggestive force posing a dynamic account of the phenomenology of the life of the mind and the nature of enquiry, this focuses our attention once more on a teacher's need to satisfy some conditions necessary for the development of such powers. Intellectual conscience, for instance, is partly a matter of moral education and all that this entails (although one can also be courageous and very nasty).

The qualities referred to as intellectual 'eros' are unteachable *per se*; but they could not develop in a person in the absence of a self-confident autonomy. This would need to be related to cognitive and affective powers of judgement, learned in the process of a broad general education which would help to ensure that the 'eros' qualities Elliott refers to are directed to objects worthy of attention. In the development of general attitudinal qualities which might transfer, such as the above, a teacher has indeed an inescapable responsibility for these are the qualities central to the development of reason and understanding, and in the promotion of moral education.

An institutional caveat

But teachers who may see the value of adopting the supportive and democratic role underpinning possibilities of growth and the achievement of transfer in their students may, ironically, be unable or unwilling to work for a common understanding in their wider institutional involvements. Mary Midgley has recently made the plea that we should renew our responsibility in academic life for 'looking for ideas in common so as to get on speaking terms again' (Midgley 1989 p.246).

Much-needed qualities of openness and generosity are at severe odds with certain negative attitudes and dispositions found in academic institutional life such as disputatiousness (as opposed to disputation!) and elevation of the negative for reasons of personal status. She refers to the distorting effects of bad intellectual habits of dispute which have a strong emotional basis. This can result in the isolation of departments and individuals within them which inhibit or destroy attempts to explore the possibilities of common ground, possibilities further undermined by the competitive 'service-station' ethos currently gaining ground in higher education.

Finally on attitude transfer, Bridges points us in the useful direction of seeking to identify what he refers to as 'context-responsive meta-competencies' (Bridges 1993). By this he means second-order skills operating at a level above both cognitive and social domains which allow us to locate a particular competence (or attitude or disposition) within a larger framework of understanding:

> The person with meta-competence has, as it were a bird's eye view of the particular competence (even while doing it) which allows them to recognise that it depends on a conjuncture of circumstances that can and probably will change. (Fleming 1991, quoted in Bridges 1993)

I agree that such 'meta-competencies' would involve the power to discriminate between contexts, would involve whatever 'cognitive equipment' enables someone to change their response between contexts, and would need to be underpinned by the attitudes and dispositions relevant to both of these, but what this above agenda could comprise is exactly the question we need to address.

The possibilities and suggestions discussed throughout this chapter – the Dewian view of attitudes and dispositions in vocational education, the still-open questions of general powers of the mind, the value of character-traits and Elliott's psychical powers – have all, I hope, a fruitful bearing on that further enquiry. So too, will discussion on the part to be played by educational processes which can impede or promote the possibility of transfer.

'Only connect'

Finally, it might be thought that many transfer problems might be solved if one was to enlist the example of the arts, which by virtue of their very nature encompass a formidable range of skills, abilities, processes, attitudes and emotions. Surely here is the area *par excellence* through which to characterise and establish transfer in a variety of senses? Many practitioners of the arts indeed *assume* this to be so; some art theorists argue it (see reference to Peter Abbs in Best 1991 p.34).

In a recent article entitled (significantly) *Generic Arts: an Expedient Myth*[1] David Best passionately rejects such transfer claims for the arts (Best 1992). More often, indeed, they are transfer *assumptions*, for as in the vocational area, it is frequently taken that transfer is too obvious to need proving. Best's argument is that specific bodies of knowledge and procedures are *essential* to characterising the distinctive nature of each art:

> One cannot discover a common characteristic, or set of characteristics which distinguishes the arts. One cannot discern some essential characteristic underlying a Rothko painting, Bach's Goldberg Variations, Michael Bogdanov's exciting production of the War of the Roses, the ballet Giselle, the film 'Babette's Feast', and Wilfred Owen's poetry. (Best 1992 p.32)

The fallacious essentialist assumption is refuted by Best on several grounds. It must be granted that it is a loose and weak definition of

---

1   Here 'generic', the grouping of x's with common structural characteristics, is referring essentially to the same phenomenon as I am discussing throughout under the heading of 'transferable'.

'common', which could be claiming that similar knowledge and understanding is being called for in the different arts cited above. Similarly, 'art', referring to all arts as a supposed defining characteristic, is only such at a *non*-significant level: there is no similarity in any *relevant* respect. And Best is right too in challenging anyone to cite any characteristics or set of characteristics which is both common to the arts and distinct from all other areas of the curriculum: imagination, creativity and self-expression occur in all curriculum areas.

I share Best's major concern, that of combating conceptual confusion in the arts. Not only is there the question of justly characterising each art as it is in order to assign meanings, values and to teach that art appropriately; one must also point out that severe damage can be done by attempts to integrate the arts. To join together craft, design and technology in curricula, for instance, can mean that the distinctive character of one – technology – may dominate the others: imagination can be played down, efficiency, measurability and standard production emphasised, and the quality of ideas can be lost as the individual and unique is sacrificed to conformity. Perry argues too that: 'the permanent importation of design... will damage the ultimate understanding by the pupil of both craft and design' (Perry 1987 p.293). Such 'integration', under whose umbrella skills, abilities and attitudes will *allegedly* transfer, can euphemistically disguise a resultant loss of understanding of what is distinctive and different. We end up with attempts to join together subjects whose commonality is either trivial or illusory. Thus calls to integrate the arts based on a belief in their generic nature need to be considered with some scepticism. But, as Best rightly argues, this in no sense damages attempts to cooperate, have a dialogue, or plan for the arts as a whole. Sensitive and perceptive common and cooperative endeavour across the arts (as in any other curriculum area) is in no sense diminished by failure to prove transfer.

Furthermore, the way the arts work with imagination, feeling and rationality may have something positive to tell us about the development of 'meta-competencies'; or, aesthetic qualities may play a significant part in other disciplines: 'there are scientists who argue that aesthetic qualities often constitute a central criterion for adopting one scientific theory rather than another' (Best 1992 p.34).

In conclusion, the idea of transferability can underpin the more general need to establish something common and shareable in the curriculum. In some ways, as I have also discussed, transfer is illusory. More is yet to be learnt about the concept: but the cooperative endeavour as described sympathetically by Best and which is needed at all stages of education is owed a higher priority while we go on learning.

References

Andrews, J.N. (1990) General thinking skills: are there such things? *Journal of Philosophy of Education* 24, 1, 71–79.

Annett, J. and Sparrow, J. (1985) Transfer of training: a review of research and practical implications. *PLET* 22, 2, 116–24.

Bailey, C. (1984) *Beyond the Present and the Particular: A Theory of Liberal Education*. London: Routledge and Kegan Paul.

Best, D. (1992) Generic arts: an expedient myth. *Journal of Art and Design Education* 11, 1, 27–44.

Bridges, D. (1992a) Enterprise and liberal education. *Journal of Philosophy of Education* 26, 1, 91–98.

Bridges, D. (1993) Transferable skills: a philosophical perspective. *Studies in Higher Education, 18, 1*, 43–51.

Conrad, J. (1902) *Heart of Darkness* (1961 edition). London: Dent.

Dearden, R.F. (1980) What is general about general education? *Oxford Review of Education 6*, 3, 279–288.

Dearden, R.F. (1984) Education and training. *Westminster Studies in Education 7*, 57–66.

Dewey, J. (1916) *Democracy and Education*. New York: Macmillan.

Elliott, R.K. (1975) Education and human being. In S.C. Brown (ed) *Philosophers Discuss Education*. London: Macmillan.

Fleming, D. (1991) The concept of 'meta-competencies'. In Employment Department (1991) *Competence and Assessment*, Issue 16, pp.9–12.

Hirst, P.H. (1965) Liberal education and the nature of knowledge. In R.D. Archambault (ed) *Philosophical Analysis and Education*. London: Routledge and Kegan Paul.

Manpower Services Commission (1985) *Research and Development paper No. 23*. London: HMSO.

Midgley, M. (1989) *Wisdom Information and Wonder: What is knowledge for?* London: Routledge.

Newman, J.H. (1873) *The Idea of a University*. New York: Doubelday.

Passmore, J. (1967) On teaching to be critical. In R.S. Peters (ed) *The Concept of Education*. London: Routledge and Kegan Paul.

Perry, L.R. (1972) Training and education. *Proceedings of the Philosophy of Education Society of Great Britain 6*, 1, 7–29.

Perry, L.R. (1987) The educational value of creativity. *Journal of Art and Design Education 6*, 3, 285–296.

Peters, R.S. (1972) Education and human development. In R.F., Dearden, P.H. Hirst and R.S. Peters (eds) *Education and the Development of Reason*. London: Routledge and Kegan Paul.

Peters, R.S. (1977) Ambiguities in liberal education. In R.S. Peters (ed) *Education and the Education of Teachers*. London: Routledge and Kegan Paul.

Pring, R. (1971) Curriculum integration. *Proceedings of the Philosophy of Education Society of Great Britain 5*, 2, 170–200.

Pring, R. (1984) *Personal and Social Education in the Curriculum*. London: Hodder and Stoughton.

Robbins, Lord (1963) *Higher Education: Report of the Committee*. London: HMSO.

Training Services Agency (1975) *Grouping of Skills*. London: HMSO.

Part IV

Community Through Organisation

Chapter 10

Creating a Learning Community on Campus

Patricia Roberts

The concept of an academic community should relate to the pedagogical ideas being practised. In the same way that pedagogy differs between institutions of higher education, so will the notion of academic community. Academic community will be affected by factors both internal and external that influence pedagogy. For example, widening access giving more diversity; enterprise and ideas of skills and capability; and adult learning, learning outcomes and negotiated learning. These notions of learning should also link to the style of academic management within the community.

The academic community in which I have worked for the previous two decades was in a polytechnic, now a 'new' university, and had a strong vocational orientation. The colleges from which it was formed had an established role in part-time courses and the student body was, from the beginning, diverse in mode of study and age profile. In the field of environmental sciences, the local community and the construction industry implicitly provided the value structure. The pedagogy which developed in my own area was problem based and that was built around the idea of the reflective practitioner (Schon 1983). As the number of students increased, personal tutoring became common practice to help maintain the tradition of students and staff working together. Student representation on course and other committees was expanded. The diversity was further increased in the late 1970s and the 1980s by access courses and by initiatives to encourage women into the construction and engineering fields. This change was partly caused by external influence but was also related to the values held by the academic community. Certainly early on it was department and faculty based. It was not set consciously within the wider context of institutional values, though these were influenced by the access policies of the Inner London Education Authority (ILEA) and resources did indeed flow into the institution in relation to this work. The separation between central and local values was also influenced by the distance between sites within the institution. With hindsight, it is possible to identify the values operating and to begin to see them articulated in the faculty plans in the latter part of the 1980s.

However, external changes to the faculty and to the institution seemed to create at the same time less clarity in shared values. Staff and students became unclear where the institution was going and over their own role within the academic community. Internal restructuring and changes in senior management disrupted the academic communities within the organisation and the change to newer or different academic communities was disruptive to learning within the organisation. The role of the middle manager in being the link between senior management and the academic teams became increasingly difficult as the articulation of the necessary, and often exciting, changes proposed was limited. The transition from a well resourced, community oriented, vocationally led academic community to a tightly resourced research as well as teaching-led community was jagged.

Having taught for two decades in this large London 'new' university I moved to a small higher education college in the north-west of England. I was attracted by the opportunity to be involved in the revitalisation of an academic community which still retained the advantages of the traditions found in church colleges. The college had expanded from teacher education into the academic studies originally offered within the teaching area, but in a very traditional narrow, discipline-based way. Recently a second vocational area, nursing and midwifery, was added. Change has occurred through the Enterprise in Higher Education (EHE) project. However, this has caused tensions and the need to re-evaluate the meaning of academic community on the campus. The nursing and midwifery being spread over a number of hospital sites as well as on the main campus adds another tension. I believe the college is moving from being a closed, caring, paternalistic, individualistic community to one which is more open, has wider values based on caring, is empowering, and is pluralist. The traditional model was about giving knowledge, care and values. As the pedagogy is revised to one more negotiated, adult and capability based, the community becomes more characterised by learning and by raised expectations and demands from both students and staff. The idea of a learning university (Duke 1992) becomes a reality in the sense of a concern with learning rather than teaching and also in the sense of a management style moving towards that enhancing the institution as a learning organisation (Burgoyne 1992). By being aware of these changes, I believe it is possible to manage the change from one style of academic community to another as a smooth transition rather than a jagged and potentially confrontational one.

Whilst this chapter is based on my current experience of a small institution, I believe it may be also relevant within a larger community. Within any organisation are levels of individual students and staff, courses, groups of courses, on up to a senior management team. In comparing larger organisations with smaller ones we can see parallels in the development of an academic community.

Below I expand on the traditional and new models of academic community outlined above and then develop the characteristics of a learning academic community. The conclusion outlines the proposed model and the way forward.

The 'traditional' model

Chester College of Higher Education was founded in 1889 by the Church of England as a teachers' training college. By 1953 it had only 153 male students and, by 1965, 550 students, including some women. Over this long period it was possible to hold the college together as a community through sheer charisma and interpersonal relationships (Ridley 1989). Ridley goes on to suggest it was a close-knit, highly disciplined community, relatively divorced from the local community and aware of its own distinctiveness. Residence was a key factor. As late as 1959 a long discussion went on over whether students should be allowed home at weekends. The mid-seventies saw expansion to over 900 and the introduction of the BEd and BA degrees (of the University of Liverpool). The personal tutorial system dates from this time with weekly tutorial slots being seen as one way of retaining the community and corporate features of the pre-expansion days. In recent years, Chester College has expanded to 4500 students in 1993, including nursing and midwifery, teacher education and combined studies degree students.

The closed, caring, paternalistic and individualistic academic community can be seen as having developed historically from the idea of the university being a place for passing on knowledge. Learned men, living in close proximity, passed on their knowledge to the students sitting at their feet. Intellectual discussion took place in the senior common rooms to which young scholars might gradually be admitted when they were felt to have absorbed sufficient knowledge and understanding. It was a process of apprenticeship to scholarly life, the mastery of a specialised discipline based on education being worthwhile for its own sake. The academic communities which developed in small colleges strongly reflected these traditions.

Within disciplinary areas there existed strong coherence of interest. Strong academic tribes are found even within small institutions.

The tutors were concerned with guarding and acquiring knowledge. They gave it to the student in measured doses and set tests to ensure the students acquired it accurately. The idea of disseminating knowledge was carried over to the pastoral care of students. This developed from the idea of acting in 'loco parentis' to young students just leaving home or coming from the environment of boarding schools. Care became seen as solving the students' problems for them, by restrictive rules about hours and behaviour and by holding their hand with the bank manager or anyone else the student needed to deal with in the outside world. The personal tutor became seen not as the academic tutor but as the solver of the student's problems whether personal, financial or, maybe, even academic. If decisions needed to be made by the student about option choices or thesis topic the tutor would seek out the student to solve the issue with them or for them. In church colleges, an even stronger tendency may have existed than elsewhere to care for the student, to take on the responsibility for the supposed interest of the student.

Paternalism towards the students was also evident within the management of the institution. The tradition of providing meant the tutors did not run the community but were left to develop their own knowledge and impart it to the students. There was little flow of information with a restrictive definition even of 'the need to know'.

The strength of this type of organisation is in the caring community being concerned about the individual. When resources were plentiful, it left the academics free to concentrate on their knowledge role without having to worry about resources. There was a sense of continuity and tranquillity. The weaknesses could be seen as the system stifling some students and not developing the student's ability to cope in the outside world. When resources became tight, it did not allow academics influence over expenditure priorities. Dependent on individuals carrying out 'duties' it exhausted some staff. It was all giving knowledge, care and values. In addition, there was little response to changes in students' perceptions as they moved through the stages of learning until some might eventually move into the research academic community.

The 'new' model

The move towards an open, value driven, empowering and pluralist academic community has in part been a response to external influences. Government policy with resource cutbacks, together with increased student numbers, have changed the nature of the academic community, particularly in the new universities and colleges (the sector funded until 1993 by the Polytechnic and College Funding Council). The 1980s expansion of higher education included mature students who did not necessarily respond to the traditional care concept but who needed support in other ways. Initiatives such as Enterprise in Higher Education (EHE) and Higher Education for Capability (HEFC) increased the linking of academic knowledge to the technological society where knowledge has to be useful. Students need competencies, skills and the capability to do useful things in the world of work (Coldstream 1993). Ideas of empowerment, capability, negotiated learning and assessment and adult learning all imply giving far more responsibility for learning back to the student.

Within subject disciplines, staff and students are trying to cope not only with these external pressures but also with the different messages on research and quality assessment. Strong traditional subject boundaries and definitions of knowledge still abound. Research into the pedagogical aspects of a subject is likely to be seen as research in education rather than in the subject area and, therefore, down valued. Tutors are thus pulled in at least two directions: between the traditional concept of developing knowledge in a narrow field and new concepts of relating knowledge to the world of work and linking knowledge across disciplines. There is less conflict in vocational or professional fields where there has traditionally been a closer link between theory and practice.

Undergraduates' experience of community in both the academic and non-academic areas is examined in research by Spitzberg and Thorndike (1992). Eighteen American campuses were visited representing a cross-section of higher education. Students, faculty, and administrators were interviewed and national surveys and other reports were also drawn on. Some of the topics studied have less relevance to British campuses, Greek life being the most obvious. However, the underlying themes of increased diversity, the role of the institution in controlling behaviour, student–faculty relations and the learning community are ones we can all relate too. Although they do not offer an explicit definition of community of their own, the authors found interviewees implicitly recognised the notion as common values, practices and goals, a sense of belonging, mutual caring and responsibility. They go on to propose a structured process for looking at and restating the meaning of community on a particular campus, through the creation of a Compact for a Pluralistic Community. This would involve all members of the community in examining and making explicit the underlying values or principles on which the community operates. The authors propose four core ethical principles of institutions of higher education (Spitzberg and Thorndike 1992 p.145):

1. Colleges and universities are, first and foremost, committed to learning.
2. Colleges and universities are committed to protecting freedom of thought and expression.
3. Colleges and universities are committed to justice.
4. Colleges and universities are committed to respecting difference.

The college or university being a pluralistic community is central to the idea of the compact. The notion of a compact is seen as strongly embedded in the American culture. The Constitution and the Bill of Rights are examples of compacts leaving latitude to subcommunities and individuals to disagree according to rules of fairness. It is not necessarily an idea which cannot be applied elsewhere. The need to be explicit in our value statements, in our mission statements and in equal opportunities policies is not far removed from the idea. Consultation may have been structured, involving wide-ranging conversations. The authors also draw attention to the need for the compact to encourage what I suggest we call 'openness' or freedom of information and which they refer to as guarding against faction and its excesses. Their examples include decisions to promote a member of staff and the criteria for accepting a student. While core ethical principles are suggested, the authors recognise that each institution's compact will be unique – based on its size, diversity, and complexity of its mission.

Another important rider concerns the preconditions seen as essential to the real implementation of the compact. This is where doubt could seep in. Would these preconditions ever operate or could we make progress while recognising the need to be addressing the 'preconditions'? The preconditions suggested are: adequate personal safety; adequate physical resources; access to required courses in popular areas of specialisation; adequate institutional services; and adequate financial support for students and for staff.

The ideas within the Compact link well to the strengths of the new model of academic community suggested earlier. Strengths include the empowering of students and staff and the development of transferable skills for the world of work. Current resource restrictions demand more consideration of how to spend funding, which is possible within the new model. The greater breadth of access to higher education creates a dynamic tension in dealing with the diversity. The emphasis on learning provides greater potential for change and growth. Responding to changes in students' perceptions of community is possible through their learning. The weaknesses include possibly seeing students (and members of staff) not as individuals. The community could become far less caring. There can be a lack of time to develop knowledge within subject areas due to the time taken dealing with new resource restrictions. There is a danger of some academic areas grabbing resources at the expense of other less strong areas. For many it will be demanding in time and energy. Conflicting values (internal and external) may not easily be reconciled.

We need a model of academic community which can take on the strengths of the traditional model and the strengths of the new model and which will reduce the weaknesses. There is a need to balance traditional values with new ones. I suggested earlier the new model might be characterised as open, value driven, empowering and pluralist. Pluralism is linked to the increased diversity in higher education. Empowerment is linked to learning and being value driven to the revised ideas of how to care, without domination. Openness is related to the learning management style of the institution. All these aspects interlink but we need to look at each in turn before coming back to the overall model.

Diversity

The diversity of the modern student body is now familiar territory. Students of conventional age have been joined by returners; a higher proportion of women is now evident even in many of the traditional male preserves such as engineering and construction. Students are more diverse in ethnic origin, though more so still in the inner city universities than on small college campuses. Students with disabilities are gradually finding their way around our campuses and onto the courses. There has also, however, been increased diversity in the academic staff. Institutions which have traditionally been teaching oriented have diversified into research and seek to attract staff with higher degrees and research records. Conversely, institutions which at one time concentrated on research have started to look at teaching expertise. The expansion of higher education has included, for example, nursing and midwifery which has brought into the academic community greater numbers of practitioners. Some staff have remained very discipline based, whilst others have widened their interests to include transferable skills and competencies. Within a college such as Chester there are probably wide religious views even though some staff will be attracted mainly by the Christian origins of the college.

The diversity of students and staff, together with external influences, has also had an impact on the curriculum. Modular structures

provide greater flexibility so there is less commonality in the programme of studies of the students. Students are less likely to spend
all their time with the same group of students or with a narrow group
of staff. Women's studies in its various forms has had an impact; from
English literature, including modules on women authors, to health
studies including modules on the particular health needs of women.
Across this more diverse programme of studies, students will also
meet a greater variety of learning methods. Modules will not all
follow a pattern of lecture, tutorial and essay even within the humanities. Working in groups or teams, self-directed learning, work-based
learning, computer-assisted learning, student-centred learning may
all now be familiar to students.

Student services have also responded to the greater diversity.
Different issues or problems are brought along to the service but the
response has also begun to change from dealing with the problem for
the student to counselling the student on how to take responsibility
for themselves. The traditional pastoral care has been referred to as
the amateur tradition, and the counselling approach as the professional (Earwaker 1992 p.101). Student diversity has also impacted on
student Unions and on the societies they support. While the men's
rugby club still exists it may well do so alongside the women's rugby
club. Other groups will be concerned with links with the local community and also the developing world. Students, many now living
off campus, will be more familiar with the diversity of the local
community and its needs. Work-based learning and community
work experience will be bringing students into closer contact with
the outside world.

So in many ways campuses are now more varied in nature. The
challenge exists, as suggested by Spitzberg and Thorndike (1992), to
create pluralistic campuses where diversity is respected but where
there is a commitment to mutual understanding. They suggest the
common thread is no more than all students sharing a common goal
of wishing to get ahead, to acquire a degree. Within that will be
numerous subgroups likened, as quoted in their book, by one vice-
chancellor to '... a Venn diagram, with intersecting circles, each circle
representing a different group with its own priorities and agenda'
(Spitzberg and Thorndike 1992 p.151).

Learning

The diversity of learning methods now found in higher education has
already been noted. The key is the talk of learning rather than
teaching, and not just the students' learning but that of everyone on

campus. Parallel, but linked, processes can be seen with the student being admitted, inducted, acquiring subject knowledge, wider skills and the ability for lifelong learning with the member of staff being appointed, inducted, acquiring subject knowledge, wider skills and continuing lifelong learning. All this activity can be seen as a learning cycle (Kolb 1984).

The greater emphasis on staff development and the introduction of formal systems of staff appraisal are part of the learning activity on campus. Appraisal is a conversation for a purpose leading to the identification of training which is, or can be, negotiated learning. It is also learning by both the appraisee and the appraiser reflecting on past activities. The university (and the college within the university sector) should surely be an example of a learning organisation. The characteristics of learning organisations identified by Burgoyne (1992) can be seen in the new model of academic community. Examples below are given of both formal and informal systems at work in academic institutions:

- a learning approach to strategy: the development and revision of academic plans, revisiting values, adapting to external change

- participative policy making: staff/student liaison committees, academic board representation and working parties drawn from across the campus

- informing and open information systems: cascading of information, team working, newsletters

- formative accounting and control: development of budgets and associated rules based on strategic and operational plans

- mutual adjustment between departments: agreeing changes in curriculum, developing joint modules within a common framework, balancing resources over time

- reward flexibility: teaching, research and administration as a shared basis for promotion

- adaptable structures: cross-department teams to progress new ideas, working parties, creation of cross-institution development posts

- boundary workers as environmental scanners and inter-organisational learning: bringing in ideas via networks and conferences, links with industry and local employers, acting as advisors, quality auditors and external examiners in other higher education institutions

- a learning culture and climate with self-development opportunities for all: staff development and training, mentoring, student learning, interchange of ideas in the senior common room

These characteristics, together with the overall concept of moving from vision to realisation to action by linking policy, operation, thinking and doing, are a desirable description of a learning environment for students and staff. Taking greater responsibility for one's own learning and participating in the learning of the organisation gives empowerment.

Values

So far, we have implicitly identified some of the values but there is a need to be more explicit about them. Mission statements have recently been seen in abundance but how detailed they are, how much consultation has really taken place and to what extent they are related to the pluralistic campus is still highly debatable. The quality debate has also had its impact on the identification of values. What kind of quality and for whom are value-related questions. The traditional value of caring also needs to be readdressed to relate it to learning and empowerment and to be redefined in those terms.

One example of explicit examination of values is Miami-Dade Community College with its development of an institutional ethos regarding teaching quality and student experience (Badley 1992). Another example is Alverno College, Milwaukee, USA with which Chester College has an exchange agreement. Alverno offers a liberal education based on eight outcomes that form the core of the curriculum. The learning outcomes were developed from the agreed values of the college and are defined within the following areas:

- analysis
- communication
- problem solving
- valuing in decision making
- social interaction
- global perspectives
- effective citizenship
- aesthetic response

Valuing in decision making is seen as a process of knowing, judging, deciding and acting (a not dissimilar process from Kolb's learning cycle referred to earlier). The way the ideas are introduced to the student derive from the practice of the Faculty themselves and their reflection and research (Alverno College Faculty 1992). On going onto the campus at Alverno and meeting with staff and students the articulation of these common themes can be seen and felt. The learning outcomes are defined at six progressive levels and each student has to demonstrate the achievement of the learning outcomes across their curriculum to level four and within their specialised area of study to level six.

Chester College has defined a taxonomy of learning outcomes for levels of work from foundation (predegree), through three stages of undergraduate learning to postgraduate learning. These outcomes include study and learning skills, competencies and knowledge acquisition within the chosen subject areas. The taxonomy has been influenced by the EHE project, experience with work-based learning (developed from a Learning from Experience Trust Project) and by the traditional values of the college.

An example of linking together values, work skills and community in the wider sense can be seen in the Physical Education and Sports Science Department. Here students are working with the Chester Sports Association for the Disabled (CSAD). Students who choose to work with CSAD can develop their knowledge and submit coursework in Year 1, undertake relevant work experience in Year 2 and do their dissertation in Year 3 in a related topic area (Cooke 1992). Another example is the values project undertaken by many of the first year students where they spend time in local organisations as well as sections of the college. They examine the implementation of agreed values as shown, for example, in mission statements. Values can thus be seen to be driving curriculum development and the learning taking place on campus.

Management

Change requires not just intent but also methods or strategies appropriate to the organisation and to the culture we want to create. We are looking for strategies that recognise the nature of academic community and which also look forward. The strategies should take account of the level of competency of academics and support staff and of the learning strategies we are trying to use with the students. They should be people- as well as task-oriented and not strategies which are going to be seen or dismissed by academics as being too industry- or too product-oriented.

Five main types of change techniques are suggested in an analysis by Huczynski (1987). These are within the areas of technical, structural, personal mechanisms, leadership and people. The technique chosen needs to be matched to the change objective or the problem to be solved. Examples for an academic community are suggested below using the change example of the need for more open communication of information:

- at the technical level by electronic mail and networking the campus

- structural by increasing representation on committees and an on-going feedback system (but recognising this may be limited at Academic Board and Governing Body levels by external requirements on membership and size)

- personal mechanisms by briefing groups and cascading information

- leadership training about communicating and disseminating ideas and information

- by people through information-sharing meetings and counselling of individuals affected by change

I suggest the influence of more women within the academic management structures has had a positive impact on using learning orientated styles of managing change. The characteristics of male and female managers may well fuse into a new style of management as suggested by Davidson and Cooper. They suggest if we define an androgynous manager as one who has the capability of being high or low in both task oriented and people oriented behaviour then we might have better managers (Thomson 1992).

Another change in styles of management generally which is very relevant to creating a learning university is the reduction in hierarchical levels. Coldstream (1993) argues the working world is improved as layers of unnecessary management are removed and responsibility is taken by educated people for their own work. The learning organisation should provide a management style that empowers its members and which is based on openness.

Conclusions

The model of an academic community which I have been proposing is value driven. Values provide openness and empowerment and recognise the pluralistic nature of the particular academic community. The competencies decided upon should be seen within the student learning and the academics' learning. At the local levels within the institution, whatever size it may be, there should be teams small enough to have an identity and an ability to work together and to take on agreed responsibilities. Overlaps between teams should be encouraged. Everyone will be a member of more than one team and membership will change as needs alter or staff and students become interested in other areas, move on to other modules. The link between the institutional level and the local teams will be based on a loose/tight fit, with devolvement of responsibility from the institutional level but within agreed rules and with monitoring and reporting back to allow the institution to review its progress.

The institution will need to keep moving forward and check its activities against its agreed values. The values themselves will need to be kept under review and will change over time. As a learning organisation, it will encourage those ideas it sees as of wider significance and will spread good practice. Ideas from outside will come in at both the institutional level and at the team level. Each team will have people at the boundaries looking outwards. The teams will be mini-versions of the whole and overlap in their areas of interest; in effect, learning organisations existing within the learning institution.

References

Alverno College Faculty (1992) *Valuing in Decision-making: Theory and Practice at Alverno College*. Milwaukee: Alverno Publications.

Badley, G. (1992) Institutional values and teaching quality. In R. Barnett (ed) *Learning to Effect*. Buckingham: SRHE and Open University Press.

Burgoyne, J. (1992) Creating a learning organisation. *Royal Society of Arts Journal CXL (5428)*. 321–332.

Coldstream, P. (1993) Will you join the dance? Education for a technological society. *Royal Society of Arts Journal CXLI (5437)*. 210–221.

Cooke, L.E. (1992) Chester Sports Association for the disabled: college-community integration. In G. Hitzhusen and L. Jackson (eds) *Global Therapeutic Recreation II*. Missouri: University of Missouri.

Duke, C. (1992) *The Learning University Towards a New Paradigm?* Buckingham: SRHE and Open University Press.

Earwaker, J. (1992) *Helping and Supporting Students*. Buckingham: SRHE and Open University Press.

Huczynski, A. (1987) Choosing organisational change methods. *Topic*, 36, October 1987.

Kolb, D.A. (1984) *Experiential Learning Experience as the Source of Learning and Development*. New Jersey: Prentice-Hall.

Ridley, S. (1989) Theological perspectives over 150 years. In G.J. White (ed) *Perspectives of Chester College 150th Anniversary Essays: 1839–1989.* Chester: Governors of Chester College.

Schon, D.A. (1983) *The Reflective Practitioner.* London: Temple Smith.

Spitzberg, I.J. Jr. and Thorndike, V.V. (1992) *Creating Community on College Campuses.* Albany: State University of New York Press.

Thomson, P. (1992) Androgynous management. In *Royal Society of Arts Journal CXL (5434),* 73. (Review of M.J. Davidson and C.L. Cooper (1992) *Shattering the Glass Ceiling: The Woman Manager.* London: Paul Chapman.

Chapter 11

Creating Community Among Teachers
A Case Study

Christian Schumacher

The case study which is the concern of this chapter was carried out in the Department of Administrative and Social Studies at a polytechnic in the north of England. The aim was to promote community among teachers by building teams of teachers around 'whole' teaching tasks consisting of integrated clusters of subject matter having meaning and relevance to the students.

The polytechnic, now renamed a university, has three Schools and four departments with 2000 part-time and 5500 full-time students. The Department of Administrative and Social Studies with 43 full-time staff offers three 3-year honours degree courses and some shorter courses leading to practical Diplomas and professional qualifications in social work.

The study covered the structure and content of the main social studies first degree courses taught by the Department; particularly the first year syllabus, which was the same for two of the degree courses. First, a survey was undertaken of student and staff attitudes towards the course structure. Second, an attempt was made to reform the structure by dividing the course into more meaningful subject areas and introducing more variety into teaching methods. Third, consideration was given to placing small groups of teachers into a revised organisation which mirrored this course structure. And fourth, plans were made to develop teamworking among the teachers in order to create a greater sense of community among them.

The original course structure
The first year degree course was taught primarily by employing four main methods. These were:

- lectures
- seminars
- essays
- background reading

Of these, the pattern of lectures provided the backbone of the course since seminars, essays and reading were arranged to cluster around the subject matter of the lectures. Our hypothesis was that the *sequence* of lectures (together with their associated seminars, essays and so on) might have a bearing on the ease with which the student learned; that a logical and chronological development of a subject was more sensible than a random series of unrelated inputs.

To recreate the experience of the students themselves in following and trying to understand the sequence of lectures during their first year, a list of the title of each lecture, together with a brief synopsis of its main content, was drawn up. Each lecture title, plus the synopsis, was then typed on a separate card. The cards were numbered and stacked in chronological order, in that card no. 1 described the first lecture on the morning of the first day of the academic year, card no. 2 the next lecture, and so on throughout the year. There were 124 lectures during the first year.

The lectures were then studied in terms of their chronological coherence. The titles of a typical series of lectures are given below. These are the lectures given during the first two weeks of the first term of the course (excluding the first few introductory lectures) in the order experienced by the students. This sequence is typical of any similar period during the first year. Readers should be reminded that the students were of an average age of 18 years, with about 5 O Levels and 2 A Levels or an appropriate BTEC equivalent:

Lecture 1	Political Culture and Socialisation
Lecture 2	Learning – Basic Processes
Lecture 3	Functions of an Economic System
Lecture 4	Philosophy as an Aid to the Social Sciences
Lecture 5	Unemployment, the Costs of Social Change
Lecture 6	Generation: the Life Cycle
Lecture 7	Human Learning and Memory
Lecture 8	Liberalism
Lecture 9	Marginal and Total Utility
Lecture 10	What it is to be Human
Lecture 11	Social Theory
Lecture 12	Transition from School to Work

These inputs, together with associated seminars and readings, are what the students were expected to assimilate in the first two weeks of their first year at the Polytechnic (and are also characteristic of the remainder of their programme)! Yet it is difficult to discern a pattern, or thread of meaning, coming out of a sequence like this. What is the explanation?

The rationale underpinning the sequence appears to be that the curriculum is *discipline-based*. The entire year's timetable is based on regular weekly slots for six main disciplines included in the Social Science course – psychology; sociology; politics, law and government; social and public policy; economics; and philosophy. Each discipline is taught on average for one hour per week.

A study was then carried out of the content and structure of each discipline within the first year syllabus. For example, the first year economics lectures covered the following subjects:

The Nature of Economics
Functions of an Economic System
Marginal and Total Utility
Supply and Demand
Elasticity
Costs and Revenues
Perfect Competition
Imperfect Competition
Factor Rewards and Income Distribution
Macro-economics: Measuring and Scope
National Income and Macro-variables
Income Determination and the Multiplier
Policy Objectives, Instruments and Analysis
Monetarism and Keynesianism
Approaches to Economic Management
Planned Economies
Developing Economies
Market Economies
Mixed Economies
Capitalism and Communism in Practice
The UK Public Sector
Sources of Government Revenue
Government Expenditure

This sequence shows a similar lack of rigour in the logic of the course construction; the approaches to the disciplines involved in the course resemble more an assemblage of loosely-related topics. Also, the written objectives of the syllabus appeared to diverge from the content as actually taught. The objectives were that the students would, to a large extent, have:

- the micro concepts and tools necessary to analyse the efficiency and effectiveness of public policy;
- an understanding of the UK government's finances;
- an understanding of the nature and consequences of government macro policy and management.

The wide range of subjects covered shows a failure to design a curriculum to meet these aims. Significantly also, a huge amount of material was being presented, despite the fact that the students to whom these many topics were being taught were not studying economics as their prime subject. They were in their first year in the Department of Administrative and Social Studies. Each of the other disciplines contained an equally large area of content. The reading list for the politics, law and government first year, for example, contained 236 books and articles covering a programme of 20 seminars and essays.

From the point of view of the single-discipline teacher, these requirements probably appeared quite reasonable. The comprehensive coverage did justice to his or her own understanding of the discipline, while an additional comfort was the fact that the series of lectures and other inputs was scheduled at regular weekly intervals throughout the year so the teacher could 'space' the inputs and see in advance how they fitted together as a whole.

But the perceptions of the students were very different. They not only experienced the teaching inputs as they occurred, that is chronologically, but also suffered a massive overload of material. Although the structure of the course as a whole was explained to them at the beginning of the course (for example, Economics Lecture 1: Overview of Course) this provided only a cursory and largely obscure glimpse of the whole. In reality, the students were only able to draw the threads together at the end of the year, when each discipline had finished telling its own story. In the meantime it was extremely difficult for them to obtain more than a fragmented picture of any particular theme or life-related topic. Karl Marx, for example, figured large in the syllabus. As a major intellectual and political figure, he has made a contribution to a number of disciplines. For even a superficial understanding of Marx's thinking, one needs to know how the elements of his overall vision fit together to form a coherent whole. Yet in the first year social studies course, Marx is briefly mentioned in lectures nos. 4, 18, 34, 41, 51, 54, 74, 76 and 109. This is but one example of fragmentation and there are many others.

Because the threads of meaning running through the course can only be woven together by memorising each part and then disentangling and reconstructing the weekly slots allotted to the various disciplines, the student's experience is rather like that of a filmgoer, who is forced to watch six documentary films cut into five-minute sequences, with five minutes of the first film being followed by five minutes of the second film, and so on in continuous rotation until all six films have been shown. It is worth noting, incidentally, that in the film industry itself a good director rarely attempts to develop more than three subplots simultaneously because it confuses the audience.

The survey

In order to obtain a measure of the extent of the students' comprehension (or lack of it) of the subject matter thus presented, a survey was carried out. The aim was to assess the degree of *satisfaction* of the students with the existing lecture sequence. To complete the survey, all the cards with the synopses of the lectures on them were shuffled and given to students who had just finished their first year. They were asked to reorganise the cards in their preferred order. The original order was concealed. Students worked in small groups. These were randomly selected from a stratified sample based on age and sex. No criteria for sequencing were laid down except that the educational needs of the students (as perceived by themselves) should be given top priority.

The results diverged widely from the discipline-based programme. The students unanimously preferred a *thematic model*, centred on clusters of recognisable life-related experiences. A comparison of the themes chosen by the different student groups showed that there was a large measure of agreement between them as to what the themes should be. Twelve themes embracing all the disciplines were shared by 75 per cent of the sample. They included the following:

Overview of the Course	Work
Human Nature	Economics
The Individual	National and Local Government
Life Span Development	Power, Parties, Electoral Systems
The Family	Models of Society
Social Class	Morality/The Search of Truth

In a parallel exercise within the case study, teaching staff in the department were also asked to sequence the cards. Interestingly the results also showed no resemblance to the discipline-based sequences the staff themselves were teaching. For instance, the first five lectures currently taught at the beginning of the second term were lectures nos. 61, 62, 63, 64 and 65. For these, the staff substituted lectures nos. 12, 108, 169, 28 and 51.

The staff's results were then compared to the students' results and further differences emerged. Most staff attempted to restructure the lectures in a logical sequence reflecting a person's lifecycle, from birth to death. Starting with the question: 'What does it mean to be human?', the staff's preferred sequence traced the development of the individual through infancy, childhood, adolescence, family, work, citizenship to old age and death.

Two preliminary conclusions were drawn from these findings. First, the disparity between the existing curriculum and the preferred order of students and staff alike was such as to suggest that a *discipline-based course construction was inappropriate for students in their first year of a social studies degree course.* Both teachers and students alike were, in their own way, advocating a framework of studies more closely linked to their own life experiences. Second, the differences between the students and their teachers are of interest. Whatever the causes, there was clearly a failure on the part of the staff to be aware of the needs of the students and to adjust the course content accordingly.

The change process

To initiate the process of change it was decided to hold a meeting with all members of staff of the Department of Administrative and Social Studies. The purpose was to share the findings of the survey and also to suggest a new approach to the organisation of the curriculum. Reaction from the meeting showed that there was much support in principle for the need to change. Everyone agreed that the course *should be* an integrated, thematic, life-related and educational experience capable of enriching and nourishing the student's intellectual, emotional and practical life.

An attempt was therefore made to restructure the first year social science course along thematic lines. Needless to say, in practice, to obtain consensus as to which themes should be included in the first year syllabus, at what density, and which should be compulsory and which voluntary, was no easy task. The debate highlighted several deep-seated interpersonal differences among the staff in interest, knowledge of the subject and value preferences, particularly between staff from different disciplinary backgrounds. There is no criticism of individual teachers intended here. The problem is historical and structural, not personal. It has been caused primarily by an excessive reliance on the academic disciplines, and the timetabling complications involved in weaving these together. This system in turn is rooted in the education of the teachers themselves, since they were also brought up in the disciplinary tradition as were their mentors. To escape from this vicious circle is not easy.

Eventually, after considerable discussion, provisional agreement was reached to examine the implications of adopting the twelve themes identified by the students. This was a pragmatic decision based on what was possible and acceptable at the time. It begged a number of strategic questions, ranging from 'Why teach these subjects in a first-year course at all?' to 'Why don't we give *all* students who come to the polytechnic a general first-year course in the social sciences?' However, we were not able to pursue these ideas further.

One immediate consequence of the decision to go thematic, was the need to rework much, if not all, of the course syllabus, in two ways. First, when the cards pertaining to each theme were gathered together, it became evident that despite the overload of information, the coverage of the theme was patchy and inadequate. Several lectures were identified which did not fit into the theme at all, and appeared to have little relevance to a broad-based introduction to the social sciences. One suspects that they might have been the subjects covered in one of the lecturers' PhD thesis! Clearly, there was a need to review thoroughly the content as well as the structure of the various course elements in order to achieve a well-rounded and holistic understanding of each theme.

Second, it became evident that the teaching process itself was somewhat one-dimensional. The menu was lectures, seminars, essays and reading, whatever the discipline or theme. Were these, one wondered, truly the best methods to stimulate the curiosity and enthusiasm of first year undergraduates? A new model was needed, and it was decided to try to stimulate learning in five different ways. First, as before, elements of the course were structured to achieve learning through the process of *informing* through lectures and reading. The purpose was to lodge information in the student's memory. Next, the process of *analysis* was encouraged; still a cerebral activity but one which taught the students to evaluate, reason and make judgements. Third, at a level of involvement which exceeds the purely cerebral, *role-playing* was introduced. In this process, the student began to 'play' with the realities being taught. Next came *skills training* in which the student practised under controlled conditions the various elements of what was being learned. Finally, students were introduced to the *real thing*, a preliminary emersion into the real world itself, a chance to carry out what had been learned. Initial secondments to projects were arranged, trainee social workers were introduced to real clients for the first time, and so on. These opportunities were to be expanded during the second and third years.

Introduction of these new dimensions of learning into the first year syllabus was a major task. Many teachers were not familiar with such approaches, having built their teaching around lectures, seminars and marking essays. At the same time they were trying to change the discipline-based course into a thematic one, as well as restructuring the course content.

Restructuring the work

The methodology to be followed to bring about the required changes was developed by the author and has been used extensively in industry and in the health and financial sectors. Known as 'work structuring' it is based on seven proven principles of work organisation and employs a rigorous and systematic process to secure their successful implementation. The principles are as follows:

1. The subject matter to be taught should be analysed into clusters of activities which together have the semblance of a 'whole' – a *whole task*. In the Department of Administrative and Social Studies the 'whole' task was to organise and run a 'whole' course, comprising interrelated and properly structured thematic elements.

2. 'Whole tasks' should be carried out by discrete groups of teachers. Groups should be of a *size* such that each teacher can enjoy meaningful social and professional relations with each other. A range of 7–12 is recommended.

3. Each group of teachers needs a *designated leader* who can coordinate the means, ends and resources of the group in its pursuit of its objective, who can lead and inspire, and who can spearhead the improvement process. The course director would fulfil this role.

4. The group and its leader should possess as much authority as possible to develop course materials, control its resources, and in general *plan* its own work. This encourages self-responsibility and empowerment.

5. The group should conduct regular evaluations and have available to it regular information by which to monitor its performance and *evaluate* its success in providing an exemplary learning environment for the students.

6. The *teaching roles* of individual staff members should be agreed in terms of holistic subject areas to be taught.

7. Group members should fully *participate* in collective decision-making processes entailing some flexibility between the duties undertaken by members of the group and the opportunity for the group as a whole to meet regularly, e.g. weekly, to share common experiences, news, plan the future, problem-solve and seek improvements in the way they work together.

When implemented together as a set, the principles create the main structural conditions for *teamworking*. A core team would be formed of full-time staff from each main discipline involved in the syllabus. Their remit would be to design, deliver and review what might be referred to as the 'whole' task of teaching the whole 3-year social science course. The team would be employed exclusively by the Department of Administrative and Social Studies (and not by their respective disciplines) under the leadership of a course Director. The intention was to take advantage of the known fact that communications and co-ordination between people is much greater among members of the same (multidisciplinary) team working together than it is between different departments representing different disciplines. If one team performed one 'whole task' there would be a 'match' between the operational interdependencies of activities within the 'whole task' and the social interdependencies lying within the same group.

Teamworking has many other potential advantages also:

- the subject area is more comprehensively covered by the combined knowledge of several minds than by an individual alone

- one student may learn better from one teacher, a second from another within the core team

- additional teachers are available to cover for absence

- social and educational contacts between students and teachers are increased

- creativity improves

- and last, but not least, several teachers dealing with aspects of the same theme can exchange experiences to their mutual advantage

On the down side, the sharing of the teaching burden among a dedicated core team raises some difficult issues for the staff involved. First, the thematic structure of the course creates the need for some selected crossing of disciplinary boundaries by members of the core team. This may be seen by some as an undesirable dilution of disciplinary distinctions (although in practice many individual inputs will remain as before). Second, a thematic syllabus undoubtedly requires some rearrangement of the teaching timetable. The regular weekly slots spaced more or less evenly over the year will need to give way to more concentrated bursts of teaching for individual lecturers, leaving perhaps more extended periods of time for preparation, research and self-improvement. This may create time-management and logistical problems. Third, teamworking will only be successful if members of the team are prepared to collaborate positively with and for each other. There has to be created a sense of community among teachers, some willingness to give and take and to share knowledge and skills with one another. This is not always easy where the existing academic culture is individualistic and competitive.

Once stable teams have been formed around meaningful tasks, with adequate autonomy and feedback, a *platform* exists for building up a *rational management structure* as a whole. Unfortunately there is not space in this chapter to describe the methodology used. Suffice it to say that the work structuring approach enables rational choices to be made as to how departments can be made to fit together sensibly, how the academic and the administrative sides of the institution can relate harmoniously, and so on.

Teambuilding

When team structures have been put in place, the task of persuading members to work together as a closely-knit collaborative unit can begin. The work structuring approach to team-building seeks to foster six *personal qualities* in team members which, if practised, can enable the members to develop psychologically and form positive open transactions and professional relationships with one another. Formal processes, including a five-day workshop, are used to achieve this. An essential starting point is to verify that each member of the group has some *belief in his or her own worth*. If people do not believe in themselves, they can rarely work as a team with others. A second condition is that there must also exist a *willingness to communicate* with other members of the team. Next, there must be a *willingness to help one another*. People will not genuinely help each other unless they trust each other. Fourth, each group member, to truly become a team member, needs to identify with the objectives of the group as a whole and not with his own particular part alone. There has to be a sense of *shared responsibility* of the 'whole task' of the group. Fifth, a *positive relationship* must exist between the *leader* of the group and other group members. This requires as much that group members are good followers as the leader is a good leader. And lastly, and possibly most important, group members need to be willing, ready and able to listen, jointly problem-solve, and especially to put aside their own egotistical preconceptions for the sake of a better group outcome which transcends their own. A degree of *humility* is essential for teamworking to take real root.

Creating teamworking among teachers is a vital precondition for changing many parts of the higher education system. When people collaborate, the potential for improvement is obviously much greater than when they do not. Teambuilding is thus an important means to an end. But it is also an end in itself. Ultimately human beings find their true fulfilment in living and working for one another, not only for themselves. This does not entail the annihilation of the individual. In a true community, each individual will find that his or her unique personal gifts can be fully developed, that in helping others one is helping oneself. Creativity and effectiveness are enhanced. Above all, it is an immensely satisfying experience.

Chapter 12

Recovering 'Academic Community'
What Do We Mean?

Ruth Finnegan

When we reflect on the discords within higher education – fragmentation between over-specialist disciplines, attempts to hive off research from teaching, competition between institutions and between departments – it is natural that we feel concerned about the apparent loss of our sense of one 'academic community'. For this sense now seems to have dissolved, leaving us with the choice, as it seems, of either nostalgically trying somehow to 'recover' it from the past or, alternatively, jettisoning it in obedience to new constraints or ideologies.

In this chapter I want, first, to unpack the concept of 'academic community' a bit further and to query whether we really have it quite right about the past. 'Community' can mean several things, some of which we perhaps have not lost at all but are developing in new as well as older ways. But, second, I will urge that there *are* significant values associated with the image of 'academic community', and that the task of translating these into the world of the 1990s – and indeed of the twenty-first century – raises significant challenges and opportunities in higher education.

A 'community of scholars': myth and reality

In the context of higher education, the immediate image that springs to mind when we invoke that emotive term community is the traditional 'community of scholars'. This image carries a series of overtones, the more influential for not always being fully conscious. It is worth bringing these connotations into the open. This 'community of scholars' is usually pictured as a close-knit personal group, probably sharing their knowledge together over a long period, the typical image often being a (perhaps idealised) view of the cloistered scholarly community of an Oxford or Cambridge college. The picture is amplified by the idea too of continued interaction between scholars and their students, within a hierarchy admittedly, but personally joined by their common aspirations for the pursuit of truth. This interaction of teaching, learning and discussion is assumed to take place both formally and informally, and in a face-to-face rather than distant context. The participants in such a community are full-time, led by the academic specialists with their own expertise and professional standards. The institutional arrangements are set to facilitate this close-knit group: not only the university courses and regulations but also the presence of libraries, residences, laboratories and teaching rooms on the spot. The whole is, ideally at least, reinforced by shared expectations and mutual appreciation: a cooperating and interactive community.

This powerful set of interrelated images has had a profound, if often unconscious, impact on how we picture a 'community of scholars'. So it is this model too that often forms the implicit backdrop to discussions about the discords of the present or about a community which needs to be 'recovered'.

The model is indeed an influential one. Even if one discounts its more elitist implications, it still informs many long-held, if unwitting, assumptions about scholarship and learning, and their 'natural' contexts. It also fits with the dominant picture within British higher education over recent generations: of the full-time student, both undergraduate and graduate, spending a matter of years in one place, interacting intensively and face-to-face with full-time teachers who themselves form part of that community of interacting specialist scholars.

But as we now increasingly realise this model needs looking at critically. Perhaps there are ways in which – like most myths – it symbolises certain shared values. But there are also some necessary challenges. I will approach these from two main directions, factual and conceptual.

First of all, it is surely clear as soon as we think about it dispassionately that this model does *not* represent the only way in which higher education and scholarship can be organised – or in fact have always been organised in the past. Even in the Victorian age – the era into which we often tend to project our idealised images – there were varied practices. In the 1880s, for example, university education included some very different arrangements from the full-time, residential, and lengthy 'community' of the ideal model. (I owe these examples to Bell 1990 and Bell and Tight, 1993) Take the case of students at Glasgow and Edinburgh universities. They were daytime students, not residential, did not have formal entrance requirements, and often did not complete a full degree for they could and did leave just with the specific credits they required for their chosen profession. St Andrews offered a special degree for women that could be studied anywhere in the world where there was a suitable invigilator: a true distance degree. The University of London and the Royal University of Ireland, furthermore, were examining boards not teaching institutions, and students had to find tuition where they could. And even in the ancient institutions of the south:

> Oxford or Cambridge professors were teaching degree-style courses to non-matriculated students not only in summer schools, but also in far-flung provincial cities. And these were taken sufficiently seriously for them to grant advanced standing in their regular honours courses. (Bell 1990)

The early women students at Oxford too – so vividly evoked in Marjorie Reeves' history of St Anne's College (1979) – may for long have been refused recognition as full members or graduates of the university. But, in practice, women studying through the Association for the Education of Women in Oxford (AEW) or as 'Oxford Home Students' were not a negligible feature of the university experience of the late nineteenth century, and many women successfully studied outside the officially recognised structure.

The model of higher education as necessarily depending on a community of full-time scholars, interacting long-term within a specific and removed locality, may have become more powerful in the twentieth century, and in the process successfully masked the prevalence of those earlier and varied arrangements. But we certainly cannot take it either as the only way in which academics can operate or as a factually-based and comprehensive guide to earlier university practices.

If our images of the traditional 'community of scholars' are more part of a prevailing mythology than a direct representation of the past, what about the more recent position in higher education? What are our actual practices now?

Certainly the *idea* that the preferred and 'natural' model consists of residential universities with full-time closely interacting students is still a common one. But the 'practice' scarcely accords with this. This picture ignores the experience of many polytechnics (only recently classified as 'universities', but for long a full part of our higher education system); and even for the traditional university sector misses some of the realities. Both in the past and the present, many students have lived far off (think of London in particular, but not just London), have interacted little outside formal class requirements, and departed promptly at the end of short terms, often to take jobs unrelated to their studies or to travel abroad. Even the famous college-based system at Oxford or Cambridge (and elsewhere) does not always command allegiance from those students who find themselves living 'out', while a close examination of that teaching system might not in all cases reveal the intense and close interaction that the traditional 'tutorial' image seems to offer – perhaps it was always more spasmodic in its realisation than we like to believe. And the numbers of part-time and mature students with their independent lives and responsibilities have everywhere been increasing, bringing new demands and new problems, and 'distance education' courses now form part of the accepted planning and public relations vocabulary.

Such practices are sometimes pictured as basically temporary aberrations from the supposedly established pattern of 'academic community': close-knit, full-time, localised, long-lasting and exclusive. Judged against that image, they are regarded as signs of failure, perhaps beyond our control, but at any rate to be deplored; or, at best, as 'problems' to be addressed. In one sense this may be true, though how we interpret this depends on our ultimate values, a point to which I will be returning. But does this common reaction also arise from our implicit addiction to the traditional 'community of scholars' myth? Is it *that* against which our current system is being measured and found to be aberrant, rather than that the current tendencies are in themselves undesirable or unnatural?

Indeed once one questions the traditional imagery and looks instead to the *actual* practices in both the past and present it becomes clear that variety and change are as much a feature of higher education as one single ideal model of academic community. The traditional myth gives a misleading guide not only to the practices but even perhaps to many current ideals within higher education. Less trumpeted though they may be, there *are* alternative visions which we must not allow to be concealed through unthinking invocation of a myth that, however powerful, we perhaps no longer completely believe in.

Academic community: alternative images and practices

Let me give some examples to illustrate these points. As it happens they are drawn from the Open University, since that is the institution I know best. But I would also stress that it is the wider implications that are relevant, not the detailed and contingent arrangements at this one somewhat unusual university.

I first joined the Open University when it was starting up in 1969. Its vision then was very different from the traditional 'community of scholars' image. It was to depend not on face-to-face interaction but on distance teaching and 'independent' learning outside the conventional university campus. Its students were not selected and set apart from others: they were neither full-time nor living in one place, and were not required to have formal entry qualifications; and they did not have to enter into a commitment for more than one year at a time. They were to be scattered all over the country, and in large numbers too. In almost every way then, the new institution was breaking with the conventional model. Small wonder that many regarded it with suspicion – well do I remember it – or at best with a sympathetic suspension of judgment: something 'odd' which still had to prove itself.

By now it is hard to recapture that sense of risk and innovation in the early years, for by the 1990s this mode of teaching and learning is more widely recognised. The Open University is accepted as an established institution of higher education with by now over 120,000 graduates and some 84,000 undergraduates currently (1993) studying its BA courses. Its students' qualifications are accepted by other academic institutions and by employers, its courses attested by external assessors, and, as with all UK institutions of higher education, it standards validated by external examiners. Success has not altered the original philosophy however. It is committed to students attaining standards of comparable quality to those in higher education elsewhere, through the mechanisms of distance learning, a modular degree structure, no compulsory face-to-face teaching, and no entrance qualification. The essential vision is of human beings and their capacity: the potential of 'lay' people, as they used to be called, to reach these standards, women as well as men (by now half of OU undergraduates are women), wherever in the UK they continue to live and whatever their age, employment or educational background.

The special features of the Open University are by now well known, but let me reiterate them to bring home again how far it is from the older image of the resident 'community of scholars'. Its members are dispersed throughout the British Isles (nowadays with not a few on the continent too). There are thirteen regional centres, and some 250 local study centres throughout the UK. Even the full-time academics are not in one place: there is no residence rule even for the 'central' academic staff, and some are in any case attached to the regional offices. Students work on their own, though each has their own local part-time tutor for correspondence tuition at a distance; any face-to-face teaching is purely optional apart from the one-week summer school associated with some (not all) courses

– and even that is not at a central Open University campus, but through a temporary arrangement with some other institution elsewhere in the country. The idea of interaction still applies but it is interacting at a distance – tutor with students; academic with course team colleagues and with course tutors and students; student with student. And it takes place through a variety of media, including the written word, telephone, radio, television, audio and video cassettes, and at times computer-mediated communication. The idea of a *residentially*-based community has been replaced by something more like a *network* of people interacting from different places.

The 'full-time' model has gone too. With the occasional exception, OU students are part-time, and successfully so (this is no second-class route). So too are many hundreds of academic teachers who fill the essential role of the personal contact and correspondence teaching for our students. The commitment to several years' continuous engagement in higher education as a price of participating in an academic community no longer applies either. In the modular degree structure people enrol a year at a time, can withdraw then return after several years, and through the complex credit exemption system can cash in their earlier educational experience into (and increasingly also out of) the OU degree structure. In the OU system, higher education has become not a lengthy commitment to some permanent academic community but a set of opportunities which people can move into and out of as suits their needs at different times.

That may sound an over-glowing picture. And of course there are the failures, constraints and controversies within the system too, many of them much to the fore as I write (such as current financial stringencies, or on-going arguments about the structuring and demands of the OU Honours degree). But the point I want to stress is this *alternative* vision to that of the traditional 'community of scholars' – a vision too that with all its problems is matched by practical arrangements already in place and working.

Let me elaborate this by taking an example from just one Open University course, the second level undergraduate course 'An introduction to information technology: social and technological issues', presented from 1988. Explaining the processes both of how the material was produced and of how it was studied by students can illustrate further the alternative version of 'academic community' I am trying to convey.

The course was prepared by a course team whose responsibility was planning and producing a multimedia distance-learning package in advance (rather than as in 'conventional' teaching modes delivering the teaching content at the time in lectures or tutorials). The team was made up not of people working permanently together, but of a network of individuals drawn mainly from two Faculties within the university (Technology and Social Sciences – not Faculties very accustomed to working together) but also from other members of the university and from external consultants. All were involved in other tasks as well as preparing the course, and given the *interdisciplinary* context, which meant presenting the subject matter in a new perspective, all also had to find time to research into the issues as they drew up the course plans. The team was far from an exclusive established group, therefore, and indeed also relied on others beside the academic full-time OU staff – internal support staff, potential tutors, practitioners in the field, external assessors. As the course neared completion, joint planning and briefing contacts were also necessary with the 70 or so part-time tutors appointed in the normal OU style as the direct personal interface with the students. These part-time tutors themselves constituted an essential network and resource both before and during the course, maintaining contact with the course team through initial briefing and later through correspondence, telephone and computer communication.

The 1500 students who enrolled to study the course in its first year of presentation in 1988 (with similar numbers in subsequent years) came from all areas of the UK, with a fair mix in age, sex, educational background and current employment. Since this was a second level course all had done at least one Foundation level course first, usually in either or both of Technology or Social Science, and perhaps other courses too. But their backgrounds both from their previous course(s) and from their other experience were variegated indeed. This in fact proved one of the strengths of the course, for, as explained below, students often shared their expertise with each other (sometimes with the course team too): some were strong on the social issues, others on the technology, some incredibly skilled in the intricacies of computer techniques or knowledgeable about applications in particular organisations. This shared expertise of students, part-time tutors and central OU staff made up a resource which contributed directly to an interactive community of learning.

The interactive element was reinforced by the course material itself – or that at least was the aim, with more or less success in its various elements. As with all OU teaching material we were attempting to deploy the distance mode in such a way as to activate the critical challenges, interactive discussion, and personal intellectual development essential to higher education but sometimes held to be a monopoly of the face-to-face teaching mode. So in usual OU style even the written correspondence units included question and answer sections, 'stop-and-think' points, and exercises to complete before continuing: one way of establishing a dialogue with the student. The audio-cassettes often carried this even further ('Switch off and do such and such before going on listening...') while the practical computing skills and the material which taught them were there not so much for the sake of technical mastery as a jumping-off ground to challenge students to consider the social and technological issues. One of the most demanding parts of the course was the personal project students had to complete on some aspect of computer-mediated communication. In this they had to bring to bear not only the academic discussion of the topic in the course material and elsewhere, but also their own first-hand experience and (through tutorial group discussion, electronic conferencing, and electronic communication of the results of their self-completed questionnaires) that of their fellow-students.

The 'dialogue' emphasis meant that taking part in the course was not just a matter of learning off a mass of 'intellectual content' from a set of powerful academics. Rather, students were actively contributing to the learning process. This meant, in the first place, that studying the course did not primarily mean regurgitation – though there was of course some content to be mastered – but more the practising and developing of such skills as criticism, interpretation, application, synthesis and (very important for the practical computer-based skills) reflective analysis.

Second, the amount of interaction was more extensive than the phrase 'distance education' at first suggests. There was of course the normal 'correspondence tuition' by which each student's seven written assignments were marked and extensively commented on by their own personal tutor. That tutor also put on three or four face-to-face group tutorials for his or her group of 20–25 students during the year – an optional not compulsory offering, taken up by only some students. The telephone was another channel of communication between students and tutor, usually on an informal one-to-one basis, but sometimes formally organised for a group in the more dispersed regions. There was also the opportunity, indeed the obligation, to engage in electronic communication. Each student was given the necessary instruction and facilities, together with university provided modem and software, to engage in computer-mediated communication with other students, with tutors, and with members of the course team both in one-to-one personal messages and in more organised group interchanges. Some of these electronic conferences and discussions were set up and controlled by the central course team, others by tutors or groups of tutors, others again by groups of students. As with any form of communication, their subject matter and aims varied enormously. Some were like tutorials at a distance conducted by students and tutors communicating through the computer screen about the intellectual issues of the course. Others were 'chat' conferences, where students could exchange news and views on topics that interested them. There were also the extensive private mail messages between individuals on (no doubt) just about any topic you care to name even if they had never met face-to-face or interacted in any other way except by computer.

Indeed, one of the most impressive outcomes was the electronically mediated sharing of expertise among the course participants. With nearly 1500 students, 70 tutors and a dozen associated members of the course team this sharing was extensive and varied indeed: from specialist technical knowledge about particular computer problems and their solutions to particular experiences in their own work or lives which could directly illuminate some particular issue currently under discussion in the course. At its best this provided a brilliant democratising means by which the many participants in any one year could share their knowledge and interchange their ideas, however widely separated by time and by distance.

I do not want to make too much of the electronic aspect – it is not common to all OU courses, has its own technical constraints, and is subject to all the familiar social and political issues that arise in any form of communication. Though innovative and, I believe, important, computer communication was only one medium among others. But the basic point I want to convey is a crucial one. This is that through a whole variety of media – printed material, personal written correspondence, telephone, radio, television, audio cassettes, face-to-face meetings, and (in this case) electronics – the participants in the course were interacting in ways which were both effective at a university level *and* fall outside the older image of the 'community of scholars'. They were not physically together, not (apart from the handful of central course academics) full-time, not operating as exclusive specialists within a fixed hierarchy nor working together over the years. When the course was finished the participants took their experience with them and moved on severally to other things. And yet over the intense nine months of the course the students, the part-time tutors, and the OU academics were able to interchange ideas and learning (as well as gossip), perhaps forge between them some shared if implicit values: some meeting of minds at least, whatever the distance. It is an alternative model of 'academic community', one no longer tied to place as in the traditional model, nor to full-time participants in a permanent setting.

Modern senses of 'community': social and academic

This alternative view of 'community' as essentially interacting *people* rather than particular *locality* also chimes in with current historical and social scientific thinking about the concept of 'community'. It has long been a loaded and debated term, of course, attractive focus for heated academic controversies. But some of the changing ideas in recent writings are relevant enough to our themes to deserve a brief comment here as a second, more conceptual, strand in our consideration of 'academic community'.

The most obvious meaning has indeed been of a *locality*. There are numerous studies of neighbourhoods or villages or areas of towns by anthropologists, geographers and sociologists taking this local sense as their focus; so too we have the tradition of 'community studies'. But there is also the other sense, coming increasingly to the fore in recent academic work, of looking at communities based not on contiguity, but on joint *interests* or on a sense of *belonging* together. Thus one can speak of artistic, occupational, ethnic or religious communities, relying on networks of people and their perceptions of shared links however physically dispersed they may be. And communities in this sense are not necessarily solid or exclusive entities, so to speak, of which people are full-time, total, or permanent members, but relative: people belong to them – perhaps transiently – for certain purposes and in certain situations.

This more open concept of 'community' now being developed is directly pertinent to our reflections on 'academic community'. Here too we can begin to move away from the earlier model of academic community defined by physical contiguity, long-term commitment over years, and exclusive full-time membership to a more open concept. We can now envisage the notions of 'part-time' or short-term membership, of belonging from a distance, and of the possibility of being at once a member of several communities.

This is not just abstract theorising, but something we can find around us, if we are prepared to look. The Open University is one particularly prominent instance. Our students – part-time, remember – are at once dedicated members of the Open University community and of the local occupational or cultural communities to which they also variously belong. And the part-time tutors, so essential to the operations of the university, are at the same time part of the Open University academic community and of those other local institutions for which many of them also work. But this model can also increasingly be applied to the world of higher education more generally. We can see its members, including its part-time and short-term participants, bring links and multiple affiliations with so many differing groupings and institutions – communities in the open sense of the word – throughout the country and beyond.

This more open sense of community gathers greater relevance too as the role of part- time and mature students becomes more visible, as credits are transferred between institutions, and as people move in and out of academic study in a process of life-long learning. So we can envisage a situation where people may be participating in a number of communities – including among these not only localised 'academic communities' but also extra-local and wider 'academic community' – in differing senses depending on their differing situations, for different purposes and at different periods of their lives. Membership of an 'academic community' thus becomes a relative and multi-faceted affair, unlike the full-time, physically located and long-term presence implied in the model of academic community from which we started.

For some the present trends represent a failure of true academic community: the result of unpleasant and unnatural pressures forced on us from outside. We have students unable to 'live in', studying only part-time, no longer with a continuing personal relation to their teachers over time; disappearing perhaps after one year or semester without any full-time allegiance to any single *alma mater*; having to juggle commitments to jobs, families or the need to earn money alongside their studies. It is true that there are certain trends within higher education today, not least current government policies, that I personally deplore. But for all that, I would not accept the view that only one model – the localised and full-time 'community of scholars' image – represents 'true' academic community. The alternative model of 'open academic community' in which people participate more, or less, depending on their purposes is equally valid. It is a model furthermore which can both give us fresh insight into what is actually going on within higher education today and also hold out a vision for the future.

An 'academic' community

What is involved in this model of an 'open academic community'? So far I have focused on the 'community' end of this concept. But it is not *any* community we are discussing. There is also the question of what we mean by 'academic'. Going back for the moment to the original 'community of scholars' metaphor, who now are the scholars? Or in the more open model of community and communities, who are the participants?

One common assumption still seems to be that scholars are to be defined as the highly professionalised full-time experts marked out and elevated within a university context for their pursuit of specialist knowledge. The content of such specialist scholarship may have widened over the years (away, for instance, from the nineteenth century focus on Greek and Latin language and literature), but the central image remains very much that of the full-time dedicated specialist, removed from others by his or her (often his) specialist standards, knowledge and vocabulary. Indeed recent anxieties about the increasing professionalisation and fragmentation of knowledge (voiced, among many others, by Ronald Barnett, see Chapter One) have highlighted this model of the remote specialist scholar and alerted us both to its reality and its dangers.

But can there be another side to this? It is helpful to go back to that other nineteenth century sense of 'scholar', meaning anyone learning or being taught, whether as schoolchild or as one of the notable 'amateur' scholars and researchers of Victorian times. This more workaday meaning – less exclusive, less full-time – helps to suggest the possibility of an alternative model in which we could regard *everyone* in serious pursuit of higher knowledge as in principle a scholar. Whether or not they are actually 'in' a concrete institution of higher education, they could all be members or potential members of an academic community.

This may sound too radical (for the moment it also leaves open what we mean by 'serious' pursuit or 'higher' learning). But in a way it is inescapable, not just as a wishful vision for the future but also to capture many of the developments already going on. First, communities are, as we have seen, made up by people not walls. Second, if we believe – as we surely do – that higher learning means personal interpretation, application and reflection by the learner and not just delivery of packaged ready-made material by specialist experts from above, then those learners themselves have to be seen as active and formative participants in their academic communities. People move round too, not only in and out of higher education during their lives, but also between institutions and countries even in conventional degree programmes, taking their learning and their own interpretations and needs with them: it is no longer a case of sitting at the feet of the recognised specialist guru in a single institution. We see credit transfer arrangements expand, new recognition for what used to be regarded as 'non-standard' entrance to higher education through APEL (assessment of prior experiential learning) and other such schemes, and an increasing appreciation that an equally normal route through higher education is by the part- time, mature and (perhaps) short-term or distance learner. Such students are no longer the inexperienced school leavers prepared to accept their place at the bottom of the hierarchy (and even *they* may nowadays have gone round the world on their own or held a job before they arrived at college). Many of our learners are now experienced adults and equals, with their established role and expertise in life, wishing to take part for their own purposes in higher learning, and with their own needs which can no longer be assumed to be subservient to those of their teachers – whose knowledge they may themselves, in certain directions, already outstrip. Through project work, through themselves applying the ideas and skills within the courses they have chosen to study, through their own interpretations of their set texts or exercises, they are themselves engaged in the world of higher learning; in the wide sense of the term, themselves scholars.

It is true that there are different levels and contexts in which one can practise as a scholar. However much we may wish to propagate the increasing democratisation of knowledge production and knowledge dissemination, it has to be accepted that some participants are more knowledgeable than others in certain respects, or more effective. But that does not undermine the point that such distinctions now need to be seen as relative, rather than absolute ones. Any single academic institution – a local university for instance – can be regarded as a community of learners-cum-scholars, facilitating a whole variety of learning at varying levels and for different purposes, whether part-time or full-time, short-term or over the years. Our concept of 'academic community' could follow that kind of insight rather than the cramped definition confining the 'true' scholars to those in some full-time, exclusive and localised community.

Is this merely a romantic vision of the future, scarcely translatable into reality? Certainly there are counter-trends, among them the insistence on specialised full-time 'researchers' distinct from teaching, departmental assertions of separate specialist identities as they compete with others, academics' reliance on obfuscating terminologies and publications to uphold their positions as experts. And many students still demand 'traditional' specialist degree programmes – and rightly so where that is their interest. But there is also the other side. Some of the older limitations are crumbling: not only the idea that the 'normal' student is full-time and a school leaver, but even the once clear distinction between 'part-time' and 'full-time'; and the Open University is not the only institution to rely on part-time staff who also hold other responsibilities. Mature and mobile learners bring their own demands – and certainly not just for the traditional academic curricula – and 'amateurs' as well as 'professionals' (if indeed that distinction is still a clear one) contribute to higher learning.

So the traditional (elitist?) delimitations of 'scholars' are now at the least open to challenge; just as was the older image of the necessarily localised, exclusive and full-time community. We will indeed, I feel sure, continue to need dedicated institutions of higher education with a physical location and a core of full-time and relatively long-stay scholars, not unlike the older model. But the aim and ethos of such institutions will be different from the older image: an academic community of *all* its learners of whatever age or economic circumstances, whether close or far, whether long-term or temporary, and with networks for its learners into the wider academic community rather than imposing walls round its own.

Values of higher learning: the need for explicitness

There is one final issue. I have been arguing for an open view of academic community which envisages it as more a network of people than a bounded locality, and suggested that *all* those taking part in higher learning are scholars, members of an academic community. But what makes it 'higher' learning or 'academic'?

This is more complex than just a question of 'level' (difficult enough as that is). It also brings us face to face with the question of values. After all, if we abandon the exclusive and local definition of community for an open one based on networks of people sharing common interests and values, we have to think all the harder about what those shared expectations are. If we meet our colleagues daily and face-to-face over a long period there may seem little need to make our values explicit: they can be left to develop unstated. But, as we also discovered at the Open University, if you need to communicate at a distance and more openly, then more explicitly expressed formulations become necessary. The same increasingly applies elsewhere, as firm boundaries dissolve, learning trajectories become less predictable and learners move in and out of institutions.

Precisely what those values consist in will no doubt remain a matter of debate. Most of us will, I presume, think they pertain to a higher and more general order than merely the obligation to deliver globules of specialist information or techniques, or to provide one-off courses, however challenging in themselves. Over and above the 'discord' of differing disciplines or competing specialisms, are there generic or longer-term aspirations we share, some common currency for our discourse? I believe such questions are not only worth asking, but even have some possible answers. One set is well laid out in Ronald Barnett's discussion (Chapter 1 of this book). He emphasises the value of transmitting the properties of rational discourse: among

them sincerity, comprehensibility, appropriateness, care, a willingness to examine matters from different points of view, and a determination to get to the bottom of things. Let me also quote the 'general
educational aims' as stated by the Council for National Academic
Awards (CNAA) – a body whose mixture of good sense and imaginative vision has not always attracted the attention from universities
that it deserves:

> The development of students' intellectual and imaginative pow-
> ers; their understanding and judgement; their problem solving
> skills; their ability to communicate; their ability to see relation-
> ships within what they have learned and to perceive their field of
> study in a broader perspective. Each student's programme of
> study must stimulate an enquiring, analytical and creative ap-
> proach, encouraging independent judgement and critical self-
> awareness. (CNAA 1991 p. 18)

I think I would myself probably want particularly to emphasise the
significance of criticism (including self-criticism) and of appreciation;
of reflective interpretation linking one's own concerns into a wider
perspective; of an open search for truth; communication and dialogue
with others; of the exercise of judgment; and, not the least, of an
enthusiasm for learning: 'delight' as Marjorie Reeves verbalises it in
her perceptive discussion (1988). I would add too, following a series
of inspirational lectures delivered to founder members of the Open
University, our responsibility to develop not just analytic thinking
but intuitive thinking too, the kind that leads to insight and discovery
(Wedemeyer 1969). None of these are exclusive or absolute abilities
– indeed it might be better to translate them as long-term and
(hopefully) habitual 'practices' or aspirations rather than by the
narrowing image conveyed by 'skills'. And no one person will surely
ever master any one of them completely. So once again, we are *all*
learners-cum-scholars within our shared academic community.

Any such lists rightly raise controversies about what should be in,
what out; where our priorities lie; and who should hold the responsibility for implementing them in this era of credit transfer and
student mobility. But the point is that these debates are now of the
essence and need to be explicit. So long as the conditions for being a
scholar and member of local academic community could be assumed
to centre on performing the rituals of delivering specialist lectures,
demonstrating standard experiments, and (perhaps) marking students' work, there was no pressing need to agonise over the rationale.
But in a more open academic community of the kind I have been
delineating where we cannot just rely on unspoken agreements, the
issues of why and wherefore, and the exploration of the shared values

of higher learning, need to take the highest profile. At this profound level, there may well be more convergence than we realise.

A 'recovered' vision?

So let me conclude with a plea that we no longer bemoan the loss of some mythical 'community of scholars', or try to 'recover' it from the supposedly harmonious past. Indeed trying to do so would be to privilege one partial model, appropriate perhaps for certain twentieth century experiences, but according fully neither with the more disparate arrangements of the past nor the developing challenges of the present. Rather we need to *uncover* and make explicit the values that we aspire to as co-members of our present-day academic community. These values, with all their debates and uncertainties, must surely inform our current vision. This needs to be a vision suited to the present but consonant with the highest values of the past – recovering and extending them through the image of an open academic community without walls, in which *all* its learners are in one way or another mutually respected, active and scholarly participants.

References

Bell, R. (1990) The Open University – Exciting Innovation or Disappointing Revival. Unpublished seminar, Open University, reported in Open House, No. 281, June, p.6.

Bell, R. and Tight, M. (1993) *Open Universities: A British Tradition.* Buckingham: Society for Research into Higher Education and Open University Press.

CNAA (1991) *Handbook 1991–92.* London: Council for National Academic Awards.

Reeves, M. (1979) *St Anne's College, An Informal History.* Oxford: St Anne's College.

Reeves, M. (1988) *The Crisis in Higher Education: Competence, Delight and the Common Good.* Milton Keynes: Open University Press.

Wedemeyer, C.A. (1969) Problems of Teaching and Learning in the Independent Learning System. Unpublished lecture series, Open University, October–November.

Contributors

Ronald Barnett is Reader in Higher Education in the University of London, and is in the Centre for Higher Education Studies, Institute of Education. His books include *The Idea of Higher Education* (1990), and *Improving Higher Education: Total Quality Care* (1992).

Tony Becher has been Professor of Education at the University of Sussex since 1975, and has served on a number of national and international bodies concerned with higher education. His recent publications include *British Higher Education* (1987) and (with Maurice Kogan) *Process and Structure in Higher Education* (2nd edition 1992).

Ruth Finnegan is Professor in Comparative Social Institutions at the Open University which she joined in 1969. She has taught at universities overseas (including the University of Rhodesia and Nyasaland, University of Ibadan and University of the South Pacific, and has published extensively on topics in anthropology and comparative sociology, especially oral literature, the implications of literacy, and higher education.

Anne Griffin is a principle lecturer in the School of Post-Compulsory Education and Training at the University of Greenwich. Her main research interests are in vocational and aesthetic education in further and higher education.

Nicholas Maxwell is a Reader in history and philosophy of science at University College, London. He has published two books, *What's Wrong with Science?* and *From Knowledge to Wisdom*, and is at present working on a third book, *The Rationality of Scientific Understanding* to be published by Cambridge University Press.

Roy Niblett, CBE, FRSHE, is president of the Higher Education Foundation and Life Vice-President of the Society for Research into Higher Education. Formerly, he was in succession Dean of the Institute of Education, University of London and Professor of Higher Education in that institution.

Marjorie Reeves is a former Fellow and Tutor, St Anne's College, University of Oxford and is now Honorary Fellow, St Anne's and St Hugh's Colleges, Oxford. She is a mediaeval historian and writer on education.

Patricia Roberts has been Deputy Principal of Chester College of Higher Education since 1992. Previously, she had lectured in planning and housing at an inner city polytechnic, including serving a three-year term as Dean of Faculty.

Christian Schumacher was Coordinator, Organisation and Development. British Steel Corporation following which, from 1979–81, he was Seear Industrial Fellow at the London School of Economics. Since 1981, he has directed his own management consultancy.

Peter Scott is Professor of Education at the University of Leeds. Formerly, he was Editor of the *Times Higher Education Supplement*. His books include *The Crisis of the University* and *Knowledge and Nation*.

Kenneth Wilson, Principal of Westminster College, Oxford, after a spell as a university chaplain and teacher, lectured in philosophy of religion and ethics. He is Deputy Chairman of the Council of the Institute of Education, University of London and is a member of the Committee for the Accreditation of Teacher Education.

John Wyatt is Director of the West Sussex Institute of Higher Education and honorary treasurer of the Society for Research into Higher Education. He has written on a variety of topics in higher education, most recently Commitment to Higher Education, a study of philosophers in higher education.

Subject Index

References in italic indicate figures.

Author Index